DR. RICHARD C. HOROWITZ

THE *Only* PARENTING BOOK
YOU WILL EVER NEED

family
centered
parenting

*Your Guide for Growing
Great Families*

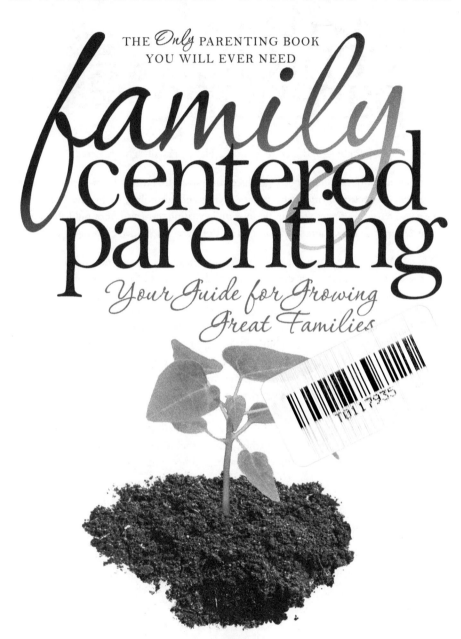

MORGAN JAMES PUBLISHING • NEW YORK

ISBN: 978-1-60037-859-1 (Paperback)
Library of Congress Control Number: 2010934840

Published by:
MORGAN JAMES PUBLISHING
1225 Franklin Ave Ste 32
Garden City, NY 11530-1693
Toll Free 800-485-4943
www.MorganJamesPublishing.com

Cover/Interior Design by:
Rachel Lopez
rachel@r2cdesign.com

Dedication

This book is dedicated to children and their parents in their search
to create and maintain an enriching and fulfilling family life.

Acknowledgement

I would like to acknowledge the many families that I have been involved with over the span of my career as an educator and consultant. Through my interactions with you I have learned so much about the importance of family life in achieving happiness.

To my children, Jessica, Louis and Benjamin, I cannot begin to express how important our relationship is to me and how much I appreciate my involvement in your lives.

I would also like to acknowledge my wife, Jane, for her understanding and love. Her support has enabled me to pursue my vision.

Table of Contents

Introduction

Children don't arrive with an instruction book. Raising children and providing for their physical as well as emotional needs as they mature is a challenging job for which we receive little preparation or formal training. Our fast paced and ever changing society has only served to make the demands of parenting even more complicated. Not only do our children remain under our care for a longer period of time but also many of the institutions in our communities are less able to support the needs of the family. In addition, in our information age era it is extremely difficult for a parent to reinforce a set of values which differs in any way from our mass culture. Furthermore, the increase of women in the workforce coupled with a tough economy has created even more stress on the family. For economic as well as personal reasons women are often torn between career and motherhood with these conflicts not only spilling over into the workplace but also producing stress for themselves, their partners and the children.

Schools have not been able to adequately respond to the strain on the family. The educational establishment is largely bureaucratic and run by individuals seemingly comfortable with the status quo. At the same time parents have demanded more involvement in school decision making and greater accountability for school quality. School people are slow to respond to changes in the external environment and continue to adhere to policies and practices which might have been more appropriate in the past. Therefore, it should not be surprising that parenting has become isolating and frustrating and is robbing both parent and child of the joy and satisfaction of this critical life experience.

We often approach parenting reflexively, relying on what we learned from how we were parented without reflecting on what we are doing. Even though we might not always be mindful of where it came from, probably a mixture of grandma and unfiltered media advice, we are operating on a set of principles about parenting that needs to be examined for its accuracy and effectiveness.

This book introduces the **Family Centered Parenting**® approach to parenting which will help parents develop their own style of parenting that is grounded in a philosophy of parenting. It will not just offer a set of guidelines, but will give parents the tools necessary to make thoughtful decisions about their parenting options that exist within a consistent system of beliefs. Since Family Centered Parenting is more a process than a program it is sufficiently flexible to be adapted to a variety of family situations—single parents, child with special needs, blended families, ranges in age of children and a variety of value structures.

Chapter 1

IS YOUR PARENTING STYLE ROOTED IN A PHILOSOPHY?

One's philosophy of parenting is not separate and apart from one's beliefs about human nature and behavior. We have certain principles about how we think people behave and how they should behave. These principles will find their way into our parenting practices whether or not we consciously acknowledge them. Our most fundamental beliefs are based in our view of human nature. For example, if we believe that people are inherently selfish, looking for the easy way out, and prone to stray from moral behavior unless fearful of punishment, then we will adopt a parenting style that is characterized by close supervision, mistrust and threats for wrong doing. Conversely, if we believe that given the appropriate environment people will tend to be self-motivated and cooperative, our parenting style will be more hands off and based on trust and teaching responsible behavior.

The organizational behavior literature provides some useful insights for understanding the connection between how a manager views behavior and its impact on workers. It is not a big stretch to compare the family with a business organization. Those in management assume a parental-like role and children are in a sense assuming the role of the worker; subordinates to the manager. Families and organizations exist to fulfill a mission and accomplish goals that are effective, efficient and which will preserve the enterprise.

Management theorist, Douglas McGregor in his book *The Human Side of Enterprise*, developed a Theory X and Theory Y formulation of behavior in the workplace which has important implications for the family. Theory X—the traditional view of the worker and working—holds that people are inherently lazy and dislike and avoid work and that those holding supervisory positions must use both the carrot and the stick to motivate workers. McGregor goes on to articulate other widespread Theory X beliefs such as: the average person is by nature indolent, lacks ambition, dislikes responsibility and prefers to be led. In the world of Theory X the subordinate (worker) is inherently self-centered, indifferent to organizational needs unless they satisfy motives, resistant to change, gullible and easily persuaded by demagoguery.

In contrast, Theory Y assumes that people have a psychological need to work and that they desire achievement and responsibility. The Theory Y viewpoint is that people strive, under the right set of conditions, for self-actualization and want intrinsic motivators from their jobs. This is a humanistic point of view that values the essential worth and dignity of others.

ACTIVITY # 1-1— *For the following list of traits indicate with a check what are your overall beliefs. Remember that you are scoring this as an overall impression and that your choice does not mean always but a majority of the time.*

A working copy of all activities can be found at
www.GrowingGreatRelationships.com

1. ___ Humans operate like other animals.

2. ___ A person is a self-fulfilling human being.

3. ___ People are inherently evil.

4. ___ People are inherently good.

5. ___ People are driven by instincts.

6. ___ People are driven by humanism.

7. ___ Coercion is the most effective motivator of people.

8. ___ Cooperation is the most effective motivator of people.

9. ___ Competition is the most natural form of social behavior.

10. ___ Cooperation is the most natural form of social behavior.

11. ___ Most people are pessimistic.

12. ___ Most people are optimistic.

13. ___ Work is inherently distasteful.

14. ___ Work is intrinsically rewarding.

(Scoring: Seven or more checks of odd numbered items suggests that you have a Theory X orientation. Seven or more checks of even numbered items suggests that you have a Theory Y orientation.)

From a cultural and political perspective, those individuals who tend to identify with humanistic philosophies and theologies probably feel most comfortable with a Theory Y orientation. Those individuals whose personal beliefs are more closely linked with an old testament interpretation of the Judeo-Christian liturgy probably feel more closely aligned with the Theory X point of view. It is somewhat ironic that adults generally prefer to be treated as if those in authority over them were oriented towards Theory Y yet they believe that they must raise their children from a Theory X point of view. However, one might reasonably ask what difference does it make if I am a Theory X or a Theory Y type person and what does it have to do with parenting?

For the first question we need to return to the management literature. Although some critics view the Theory X—Theory Y dichotomy as oversimplified, most researchers have concluded that workers under a Theory Y supervisor are more motivated and more productive. In addition, it is felt that the worker passivity associated with Theory X organizations is a product of Theory X management practices rather than a natural condition. In fact, the large scale efforts in corporate America to increase participatory management and team building in the workplace are predicated on the effectiveness of a Theory Y orientation.

To establish the link between Theory X and Theory Y and the family we need to look a little deeper into what Theory Y is really telling us about motivation and human behavior. In the structure of the family, it is reasonable to see parents as equivalent to managers and children as equivalent to workers or subordinates. Management, in the industrial setting, is responsible for organizing the elements of productive enterprise—money, materials, equipment, people—in the interest of economic ends. In the family, parents are responsible for organizing the elements of a productive family enterprise—money, intellectual and moral capital (equivalent to materials and equipment), equipment (clothing, cultural & educational resources) in the interest of successful family life.

It is important at this point to make sure that we understand the equivalent of economic ends in the family context. In the business world, a successful organization is measured by bottom line results—profits. In the family, if we think about it, success is measured by the degree to which our children develop intellectually and morally and function harmoniously within the structure of the family. Under the leadership of their parents, children need to be responsible decision-makers that will enable them to achieve their potential and lead fulfilling lives.

Therefore, it is worthwhile to look more deeply at Theory Y management practices to learn how we can translate them to the parenting practices. Theory Y holds that the motivation, the potential for development, the capacity for assuming responsibility, the readiness to direct behavior toward organizational goals are all present in people. Management does not put them there. It is a responsibility of management to make it possible for people to recognize and develop these human characteristics for themselves. In addition, the essential task of management is to arrange organizational conditions and methods of operation so that people can achieve their own goals best by directing their own efforts toward organizational objectives. This is a process primarily of creating opportunities, releasing potential, removing obstacles, encouraging growth, and providing guidance. It does not involve the abdication of management, the absence of leadership or the lowering of standards.

Just substitute the word parents for management and we can begin to see the parallels between effective organizations and effective families. Remember, for the moment, to focus on the long-range goals of parenting rather than the issues involved with day to day compliant behavior. To paraphrase, the role of parents is to arrange conditions in the child's environment so that children can achieve their goals by directing their own efforts for personal growth and the welfare of the family. This is an on-going process which asks the parents to create opportunities, remove obstacles, encourage growth and provide guidance without giving up the leadership or lowering of standards by the parents.

A useful analogy to help us understand the Theory Y approach to parenting is based on the job descriptions of two very different occupations, the engineer and the shepherd. The role of an engineer is, under a set of limitations governed by available resources, to carefully analyze, plan, develop and evaluate the concept of a desired function into the reality of a finished product. The successful engineer must micromanage the process with constant correction and attention to detail. An effective process for producing a better refrigerator or computer but not necessarily the best approach to guiding a family. If we attempt to engineer our children we have tacitly adopted a Theory X role in parenting. On the other hand, the shepherd's job is to find a safe place for his/her flock that contains adequate potential for finding food. The shepherd does not mingle with the flock but remains at a distance observing the beasts' natural proclivities. He monitors the flock and adjusts the process only when necessary. In addition, she must remain vigilant to make sure that predators are kept at bay. The shepherd does not need to supervise every step of those processes which will be taken care of by nature and/or are out of his/her control. In other words, the shepherd is applying a Theory Y approach to the job at hand.

Sounds promising? But before we continue with a Theory Y conceptualization of parenting we need to be really certain of what common parenting practices need to be examined and discarded. The following exercise should be helpful.

ACTIVITY # 1-2— *For each of the following statements indicate if you think it is a Theory X parenting approach or a Theory Y. Mark each statement with an X or Y accordingly.*

A working copy of all activities can be found at
www.GrowingGreatRelationships.com

____ 1. Spare the rod and spoil the child.

____ 2. Ultimately, parents are the bosses and the children must do what they say.

____ 3. Negotiating with a child is a sign of weakening parental authority and should be avoided.

____ 4. Giving children money for good grades and other accomplishment is good preparation for real life.

____ 5. A parent's role is a more like a police officer than a coach.

____ 6. A parent's authority increases as a child's power is limited.

____ 7. A child's temperament should not be considered in making parenting decisions.

____ 8. Being a good listener, including validating a child's feelings, is not an essential part of the parenting process.

____ 9. Discipline and punishment are the same things.

____10. Getting good grades is the most important goal for a child's education.

(Scoring—If you marked only X for all of the questions you are correct. These statements were designed to illustrate Theory X beliefs and practices and to serve as an additional means for self-examination of one's parenting philosophy).

Let's take each of these statements and subject it to analysis. "Spare the rod and spoil the child" is an adage which implies that a physical punishment from a parent is necessary to avoid a spoiled—read overly indulged and irresponsible—child. The assumption is clearly grounded in Theory X beliefs that harsh punishments are necessary to control behavior. To begin with, utilizing physical means to punish or control is by definition corporeal punishment. There are several problems with corporeal punishment. First we are sending our children a message by parental modeling that physical aggression is a legitimate approach to problem solving. In other words, when we are displeased with another's behavior we are justified in hitting. Second, a swat or a slap does not insure that a child is taking responsibility for his/her behavior. Once the sting is gone and the crying stops there is usually no follow-up. Children become used to the process. They take the short-term pain and go about their business with little attention actually directed to the reasons for the misbehavior. Moreover, the humiliation that frequently follows from being physically overpowered and intimidated reduces a child self worth. Finally, as children get older and bigger it requires more and more physical force to inflict sufficient pain to get their attention. This opens up issues of child abuse and the potential for highly destructive physical confrontations, especially during the teenage years, between parent and child.

The next statement in the activity deals with the very nature of parental authority. Parents are legitimately better able to understand the business of living by virtue of the wisdom they have hopefully acquired through learning from life's lessons. The challenge is to bring that wisdom to the parenting arena without imposing it in an overly authoritarian manner. One might ask, "What is the matter with authority? Children should learn to respect rules and the rights of others." Granted, but let us not treat authority and authoritarian as synonymous. The notion of authority, defined as the force which brings adherence to established rules and regulations, is fundamental to human social behavior. Humans intrinsically accept the notion that there must be an orderly system to govern social interactions when certain conditions are met and that they will generally adhere to this system by following established rules with little external prompting. However, how those rules are established largely dictates the means by which those rules and conventions are enforced. If rules are perceived as equitable and consistent with the values of the community, and if those rules are formulated with input from those that are affected by them, compliance becomes less of an issue. Under these conditions, authority flows naturally with little need to impose it through coercive measures. Coercion is getting someone to do what you want them to do regardless of their preference or inclination. It can be achieved by real or threatened use of physical force or by a system of rewards and punishments designed to manipulate another's behavior.

The natural flow of authority is at the heart of participatory Theory Y management which, when implemented with integrity, has been proven in the business world to be the most successful leadership/management style. In family life adults, by virtue of their acquired wisdom, should take a leadership role in the rule making process. Leadership does not mean imposition. It means that parents should **manage** the rule setting process in a way that ensures participation by the children with clear explanations and illustrations of how those rules will benefit all members of the family. In the coming chapters, the process of rule setting will be illustrated more completely.

The next statement addresses the issue of negotiating with children. The Theory X parent looks upon negotiation as a sign of weakness which will be exploited by children to weaken parental authority. The imagery of the child whining and making excuses to avoid consequences from negative behavior is what probably comes to mind. Let us re-frame the concept of negotiation. Negotiating is a means of getting our needs met through a process of verbal give and take. When done properly, it affords parties in a dispute with a means, usually verbal, to achieve a workable arrangement that is mutually satisfying or at least livable. As adults we rely on our negotiation skills on a daily basis to get our needs met in an appropriate manner. At work, at home, in the community and with friends, strangers and family, we utilize our negotiation skills to navigate our way through a multitude of situations. If we accept the fact that being a good negotiator is an important life skill for an adult, we must then ask ourselves, "What is the best way for my child to learn this skill?" The answer is the same for any skill we need to master. Learn by observing those modeling successful techniques, try it out ourselves, respond to constructive feedback and continue to practice to improve. Therefore, as parents we must model effective negotiating skills. We do this by utilizing communication techniques, encouraging our children to negotiate, providing constructive feedback, and praising their growing mastery.

Statement number four deals with the imperative to provide tangible, external rewards as a means to guarantee compliance with standards. The Theory X parent or manager relies heavily on this behavior modification technique to encourage performance believing that without outside motivators people will just slack off. There is no doubt that this type of reward may increase repetition of a particular task. However, there are serious consequences. Motivational studies suggest that money alone is insufficient to motivate optimal performance. Money, or similar tokens for younger children, may maintain a certain level of performance but will rarely propel individuals to excellence. The reason being that money in of itself is not a primary need satisfier. It might help individuals acquire greater material comfort but, especially with children, misses the mark in fulfilling more basic needs. In addition, tangible rewards require constant change or increase to effectively serve as motivators. Children become increasingly demanding about the quantity and quality of our rewards requiring us to up the ante to maintain their power. Finally and most importantly, reliance on extrinsic or external motivation diminishes the intrinsic or internal pay off for success. Do we want our children to earn good grades or do we want them to be self-motivated learners with inquiring minds who learn because it is a satisfying feeling to acquire the power of knowledge? Our brains do not need to be taught to learn about the world, learning is a natural process that is best encouraged by the positive feedback received from acquiring mastery of new skills and concepts. Reliance on externals just further reinforces the worst aspects of our formal system of education—learning only what will be measured by a particular test. This is best illustrated by the perpetual question of the student, "Will this be on the test?" If it isn't on the test there is no need to learn it.

Statement five, "A parent's role is more like a police officer than a coach," defines an essential belief of Theory X supervision. A cop's role is to catch people doing something wrong or deter them from wrong doing by reminding them of the possibility of being caught. The "gotcha" mentality of parenting assumes that children will do wrong without close and constant monitoring. There are several problems with this idea. From a practical standpoint we simply do not have the ability to closely supervise our children as they begin to go out into the world. Even in school settings, the ratio of adults to children makes constant monitoring an impossibility. Therefore, if we do not help our children to self-regulate, they will far more likely indulge in unsafe or inappropriate behaviors when the boss (parent or teacher) is not watching. Children who develop self-regulatory systems and achieve a high state of moral development, know right from wrong and can usually make good choices about their behaviors when adults are not watching. Furthermore, making positive choices without constant adult reminders empowers a child by building their self-efficacy. That is an inner belief that they can be successful and have control over their environments.

A coach's role is different. The coach is clearly an authority figure representing standards of behavior and performance. However, unlike the cop, the coach's primary goal is to assist growth and improvement, not to punish mistakes. Coaching is an action-oriented partnership that concentrates on reaching goals relying on verbal guidance and frequent verbal feedback to achieve success. It is positive because it focuses on future performance rather than errors of the past and is more compatible with parenting than policing because of its reliance on modeling and communication skills. Being effective in these skills requires a relationship between parent and child built on a foundation of caring, trust and mutual respect. Who would disagree with the importance of these elements in the lives of our families? Not only do strong relationships have short-term payoffs in helping to create a harmonious family life, but it also lays the groundwork for the evolution of the parent child relationship into the child's adulthood. We are far more likely to want to spend time with our favorite coach from our childhood than the cop who constantly sought to catch us doing something wrong.

Statement number six deals with the concept of power. In the next section, the consideration of power as an essential human need will be discussed at length. At this point let us define power simply as the ability to influence one's environment. For those individuals in custodial type positions with children such as teachers, scout leaders, youth workers and parents, power is defined as controlling the behavior of clients (children). If we conceptualize power as a finite quantity then if one wants more power it has to come from someone else. For illustration, think of a pound of power existing in a closed system. If you have a half-pound of power and your client has a half-pound and both parties are satisfied, we are in good shape. However, if one party needs more power to feel satisfied, the only place they can get it is from the other individual. Most likely the other person would be unwilling to give up any of his half pound just to satisfy someone else's needs. Therefore, for the individual needing the extra power he will attempt to take it away from the other person who will not willingly yield. That is the essence of a power struggle that never ends. The person who lost power will resent the winner and constantly seek to restore power by struggling with the winner or finding someone else to bully into giving up power with all the related negative consequences.

However, if we view power as an abundant resource not confined to a closed system we can see that one can obtain more power without taking power away from another. In other words, we can empower without overpowering. As parents, if we are able to parent with minimal stress and are able to derive satisfaction from having done a good job we will feel more powerful. If we create and manage family systems which allow a child to feel mastery in her life, with its concomitant elevation of self-esteem, that child will not need to rely on oppositional and self-destructive behaviors to feel powerful. Therefore increasing a child's power will not only not diminish a parent's power but will also empower the parent.

Statement seven seeks to underscore the importance of appreciating individual differences. The Theory X parent or manager believes that we are all essentially similar and that one size fits all when it comes to compliance and supervision. This style ignores the many shades of gray that lie between black and white. The Theory Y parent or manager accepts the fact that there is nothing more unequal than the equal treatment of unequals and understands that a child's temperament will often dictate the approach used in problem solving. Recent research on human personality has suggested that between 40 to 60 percent of our temperament (personality characteristics) is with us at birth. Traits such as introversion—extroversion, risk taking and level of arousal are apparently hard wired in our brains. That is not to say that environment doesn't have an influence as to how these traits are expressed and the degree to which they fall on a trait's continuum. However, if your child is introverted, do not try to make them the life of the party. Accept the fact that their alone time might be perfectly comfortable to them and they may only need a few close friends rather than a larger social group. Temperament becomes a particular problem when there is a significant mismatch between parent and child. In these situations a parent has to be especially mindful to respect the fact that their child's personality is unique and may be different from their own style of behavior. A particular temperament is neither right or wrong.

The next statement focuses on a specific yet extremely important communications skill, being a good listener by validating the feelings of another. In Chapter Two we will explore and have an opportunity to practice communication skills. At this point, part of the Theory Y parenting package is the belief that we can build relationships with our children that are based on mutual respect and understanding. One of the ways to get there is to be a good communicator. As a starting point, if we model effective communication skills then our children are more likely to practice them. Specifically, communicating begins with listening. The verbal and non-verbal feeling messages that our children send need to be acknowledged and validated as a prerequisite to problem solving. By validating—which does not necessarily mean agreeing— we merely accept that the feeling state being communicated is legitimate for that individual. For example, if a child is crying because his friend called him a name we have several reply options. One common response might be to tell your child it's only a name or, "Bobby didn't really mean it." Despite the fact that a parent might view this as an attempt to soothe the child's feelings, it is not a highly effective response. It is suggested that a parent open the conversation with an acknowledgement. "You look really sad, because of what Bobby said. What can we do about it?" This second approach values the sad feelings of the child. From an adult perspective these feelings might be out of proportion to the event. But to the child they are real and should be valued. After the validation, an invitation to problem solve is offered. This sets the stage for dealing with the issue permitting the parent-coach to provide guidance in the problem solving part of the process. In addition to setting the stage for fixing a problem, validation increases the self- esteem of the child.

It demonstrates that they have been listened to and that their feelings are important, essential ingredients for empowerment.

Statement nine deals with whether or not discipline and punishment are synonymous. Theory X would label them as essentially the same, Theory Y makes sharp distinctions. The following activity should help clarify the differences.

ACTIVITY # 1-3— *Place a "P" next to the phrase or sentence which you would associate with punishment and place a "D" next to the phrase or sentence which you would associate with discipline.*

A working copy of all activities can be found at
www.GrowingGreatRelationships.com

---

1. _____Expresses power in terms of personal authority.

2. _____Consequences that vary and are determined by situational factors.

3. _____Rules that are negotiated between parent and child.

4. _____Grounded in terms of retribution or revenge.

5. _____Right or wrong with little in between.

6. _____Is imposed upon or done to someone.

7. _____Concerned with now or the immediate future.

8. _____Responsibility is assumed by individual who commits the infraction.

9. _____Options are kept open for individual to choose to improve behavior.

10. _____An active process involving close sustained personal involvement.

11. _____Diminishes self-esteem by shaming the individual.

12. ____Emphasizes teaching ways to act that will result in successful behavior.

13. ____Responsibility is assumed by the one in authority.

14. ____Can be friendly despite the fact that there are unpleasant consequences.

15. ____Expedient.

16. ____Often creates a desire to get even.

17. ____Anger towards the individual rather than the act.

18. ____Short term with little personal involvement.

19. ____Challenging and time consuming.

(Scoring—Items 2, 3, 7, 8, 9, 10, 12, 14, 19 are associated with the practice of discipline with the remainder associated with punishment.)

The common theme is that punishment, although expedient, tends to diminish the self-worth of the individual receiving it while simultaneously shifting responsibility from the "punishee" to the "punisher." This reduction in responsibility often leads to repetition of the punished behavior or other similar behaviors which might be inappropriate. In addition, an unintended consequence of punishment is the granting of power to the "punishee."

This often happens when children are participating in a behavior control system, which requires earning points to gain tokens, privileges or achieving levels. The children who have the hardest time earning points tend to give up entirely and receive power from a negative identity as a permanent resident of the lower tier. They earn status as an individual who is beyond punishment. Teenagers who wind up incarcerated in detention facilities often return to their peer groups as heroes. They have been punished and survived thereby elevating their status.

Another problem with a punishment orientation is that it is often connected to an emotional response. Parents have a tendency to become more punitive when they themselves are angry. If your 13-year-old doesn't come straight home after baseball practice and you are sitting home worried sick, when he does appear with some flimsy excuse, you very well might resort to consequences that are extreme including emotional or physical abuse. These feelings arise out of a parent experiencing a loss of control that leads to anger. When one is angry, the more reflective and analytical portion of our brain shuts down and we resort to our more primitive flight or fight responses. This process is called "downshifting" by cognitive theorists and goes a long way to explain why we regret our acting out behaviors after the fact. However, if we take a little time between the child's transgression and the discussion of consequences we give the child and ourselves an opportunity to reflect upon the situation and agree or at least accept the consequences of his/her behavior. Processing can only occur when we have reduced the angry feelings and allow the thinking part of our brains to function.

Conversely, discipline is often more challenging and time consuming because of the need to engage in discussion and processing. The only way for a child to truly take responsibility for his behavior and commit to changing that behavior is through dialogue and coaching.   However, since following the principles of discipline will most likely reduce the number of misbehaviors, in the long run it should prove less stressful and time consuming than purely punitive interventions. Being a good disciplinarian requires a constellation of skills and techniques which a parent needs to learn. In the following chapters, learning and perfecting these skills will be explored.

Statement ten, the last item in our belief survey, deals with an issue where a parent only has control over the consequences of the process. The practice of grading is not within the discretion of a parent, but rather a product of our educational system. Educators also struggle with the Theory X—Theory Y paradigm in the way they control student behavior and monitor student performance. Grading, as it is implemented in most school systems, is clearly a Theory X practice since it relies on external rewards to motivate. Although positive reinforcement from those we value—parents, teachers and peers—is important, excessive dependence on the external leads one to rely on the symbol more than the underlying substance. In other words, students begin to work for the grade rather than for the satisfaction of acquiring new knowledge. As indicated, schools issue grades and this is not an issue a parent controls. Therefore, let us not place additional emphasis on the grade beyond what our schools are already doing. Parents should re-focus our attention to the quality of our children's learning and reinforce the new skills and creative thinking that results from mastering the content and concepts of our children's school experiences.

If one accepts the point of view that punishment, coercion and overly authoritative Theory X parenting approaches are not effective, and that as adults we prefer working under the leadership of Theory Y bosses, then we must find a way to implement a Theory Y approach at home. However, before we get to the implementation stage of Theory Y parenting, we need one more piece of theory to help us solidify our philosophical foundation. We need to reflect and incorporate into our parenting practices our understanding as to what fundamentally motivates behavior for children and adults.

All Behaviors Are Choices

Dr. William Glasser a renowned psychiatrist and educator has developed a theory of human behavior based on basic human needs. Glasser, the founder of "Reality Therapy," developed a needs oriented theory of human behavior originally named "Control Theory" and later refined under the name "Choice Theory." The theory is a simple but elegant attempt to explain the origins of both the psychological and physical behavior of human beings which he calls "total behavior." Total behavior is made up of four components. They are: acting, thinking, feeling and the physical reactions which always come with the other three components. Acting and thinking are always voluntary; feeling and physical responses can only be changed through changing how we act and think.

Glasser used the term Choice Theory because he believes that all behavior is chosen and all the choices we make are an ongoing attempt to act on that real world so that it coincides with a small, simulated world that we build into our memory. This inner world is our "quality world" and is central to our lives. We are always in the process of modifying it so that it reflects what we need right now. We build it, starting shortly after birth, from all we have perceived that feels good. What feels good is anything that we do that satisfies, or seems to satisfy, one or more of our five basic needs that are built into our genetic structure. These needs are **survival, love and belonging, power, freedom and fun.** Unlike other needs theory, Glasser does not believe these needs are hierarchical. Hierarchical is when we need to satisfy a lower level need before we can move on to a higher one. Sometimes our behavior satisfies the need bringing a positive flow of emotions and physiology. At other times our behavior, albeit our best attempt at that moment to meet the need, is less successful and creates negative emotions and physical reactions. The conclusion is that all behavior is internally motivated.

Let us take a look at each of these needs and see how it operates in our lives. Glasser views survival on a rather primitive level (food, clothing, shelter, safety). Although of equal importance as the other needs, in our culture, for the most part this need is met. Therefore, in order to understand behavior for children and adults we can assume that meeting our survival need is relatively straightforward and does not create negative emotions and physiology. However, since the tragedy of 9/11 and the national "War on Terrorism" we cannot dismiss the potential diminishing of our fulfillment of the need for safety as a possible source of behavioral choices.

Love and Belonging represents the need that defines our social relationships. affiliation, friendship and intimacy are examples of love and belonging. We strive to meet this need in all aspects of our daily living. In our families, community groups, work environments, schools, houses of worship or at any other informal or formal grouping of people, the drive to be cared about, nurtured, and to form bonds with others is a significant motivator of our behavior. For example, a person might choose a particular church to attend on Sunday. Although our primary stated reason for going to church is to worship God, if one does not feel accepted by and affiliated with the other congregants a person will probably find reasons not to go and eventually find another church. In other words, if the need for love and belonging is not met, even if on the surface it was not our primary motivator, we will experience discomfort that will be expressed in negative feelings. These negative feelings, in turn, lead us to make different choices in our attempt to fulfill our needs.

Freedom is our ability to make choices and decisions. The need to move freely and express oneself freely and the ability to choose how we spend our time is also an essential driving force in our lives. A negative example might be helpful in further clarifying how this need operates. Procrastination is a behavior most of us indulge in on an at least occasional basis. For some individuals it becomes chronic and highly dysfunctional in their lives. Choice Theory tells us that procrastination is a behavior we are choosing at a particular moment because it is our best attempt to meet our need for freedom. Avoidance of a task or responsibility is in effect a choice not to take action. In other words the procrastinator is meeting his/her need for freedom. Even though there may be negative consequences for this choice, unless the need for freedom is met in some other way, the procrastination will persist.

Fun, the need for enjoyment, satisfaction, laughter, humor and recreation has been undervalued for parents in our highly competitive fast paced world. This is particularly troubling as evidence emerges that laughter and humor are important in reducing stress and enhancing our immune system. Parents tend to diminish this need and perceive its attainment with a degree of guilt. In their minds they have placed having fun as subordinate to being good (read powerful) parents.

A great illustration is a recently viewed bumper sticker on a mini-van that stated, "I Don't Have A Life, My Daughter Plays AAU Basketball." The message is that being a dedicated parent means we must sacrifice our own needs as adults. Children also have far less opportunity for the pure fun of spontaneous play in a culture that erodes childhood by exposing children to organized activities at younger and younger ages. It is no wonder that alcohol and drug abuse, promiscuity and countless hours glued to mindless forms of entertainment have become so entrenched in our everyday lives. These behavioral choices reflect our best attempts to meet our need for fun, again, despite the apparent negative consequences.

The last need, and probably the most significant in the parent/child relationship, is the need for power. Power is defined as one's ability to influence one's environment—a sense of control and importance. It is also expressed as feeling capable, being respected, being recognized, receiving attention and summarized in the broad concept of self-esteem. Clearly, meeting our need for power as parents while dealing with our children's needs for power is often at the root of most family problems. Children who have disabilities or who find themselves out of the mainstream have great difficulty getting their power needs met through conventional behaviors and will often choose more deviant behaviors as their best attempt to meet this need.

At this point it is important to understand that a given behavioral choice will be experienced differently by individuals. The reason for this goes back to the notion of the quality world each of us has constructed. Meeting our needs with positive emotion and physiology occurs only when the consequences of our chosen behavior are congruent with our mental picture (quality world) of successfully meeting our need. Since our quality worlds are unique a need fulfilling choice for one might be experienced very differently for another. Needs are truly met only when the consequences of our behavior match our quality world picture.

Examples might help illustrate how our quality world shapes our responses:

Frank Jones is a 40-year-old head of household earning $65,000 per year. His wife, Sharon, earns $25,000 working part time. They have two school age children, live in their own home and have a reasonable mortgage. Frank participates in a 401K program at work and has started a college fund for the children. They have little credit card debt and one of their automobiles is fully paid off while the other has several modest monthly payments remaining. Frank is fixated on money. He has his computer on constantly tracking the stock market. He reads the financial section of the newspaper obsessively and subscribes to several financial newsletters. His worrying about financial security is detracting from the quality of family life. At his daughter's soccer games he is so absorbed in making decisions about moving his money among his various mutual funds that he barely notices what is happening on the field. Frank is not sleeping well and has been increasingly careless about attending to maintaining the home. Sharon feels she must remind him constantly to mow the lawn and to *take care of needed repairs around the house. She is growing resentful and just can't figure out what is wrong.*

The Choice Theory perspective would tell us to approach this issue by focusing on Frank's behavior, not on Frank's emotion (anxiety) and physiology (sleeplessness). The problem behavior is Frank's procrastination. The first question to ask is, what need is Frank attempting to meet through procrastination? Looking back at our list of basic needs, we can safely assume that procrastination is linked to a need for freedom. Putting off his attention to necessary chores is his way of feeling that he has a choice in how he is spending his time. The fact that there are negative consequences (Sharon's unhappiness) for this behavior and that his anxiety and insomnia persist means that although his choice of behavior is his best attempt to meet his need for freedom, it is not successful and the pattern will surely continue. The next step would be to work with Frank in identifying the features of his inner or quality world that define freedom. These criteria are unique to Frank and have been shaped by his life experiences. Frank verbalizes that financial independence, as he sees it, is at the essence of his quality picture of freedom. He goes on to specify that having enough capital to pay for his children's education and sufficient investment income to retire at age 55 is what he requires. Furthermore, he needs to have it in place right now. Despite an outsider's perception that Frank is in good financial shape, his unique standards which form his quality world picture of freedom are not being met. The next step in working with Frank would be to have him examine the accuracy or reality of his quality world picture. The goal would be to have Frank modify his quality world by examining and utilizing the evidence of his current financial position in order to reconstruct a more realistic timeline for achieving his financial goals. When he accepts that where he is at age 40 is freedom for this stage of life, his behavior would no longer be totally absorbed with meeting his need for freedom. The procrastination would stop, his inordinate time worrying about money would diminish and his emotions and physiology would improve as his family responds positively to his availability.

Another useful illustration concerns Larry.

Larry is a sixth grader of above average intelligence who has a learning disability that has affected his school progress. He generally earns C's in reading and language and C's & B's in his other subjects. He has been classified as in need of special education services since the beginning of the third grade and receives extra help in reading and language arts. He also has been diagnosed with ADHD and has been taking Ritalin for the last two years. His ADHD has had an impact on his relationships with peers and Larry has become increasingly isolated from friends. Larry is sometimes difficult to parent but up to now he has done fairly well in responding to his parents and relating to his older sister. Larry's mother receives a telephone call from school indicating that she needs to leave work and pick up Larry at school. Apparently, he got into an argument with a classmate and when disciplined by the teacher he directed profanity towards her. Larry was sent to the office to see the assistant principal. He again used profanity and verbally threatened the assistant principal. The school placed Larry on a three day out-of-school suspension. Larry's mother is angry about having to leave work in the middle of an important project. When she enters the school she feels embarrassed when she gets that "look" from the school secretary. The assistant principal is clearly upset with Larry and hands him over rather unceremoniously to his mother with a reminder that a conference will be held upon Larry's return to school. Larry's mom attempts to discuss the situation with Larry on the way home. She raises her voice in frustration and he responds in kind. He states that he is angry with the teacher and says that he is being blamed for someone else's behavior. He says that he wants to beat up another student in the class and that the teacher is picking on him. He calls the assistant principal an "asshole" and says he would like to blow up the school.

The chart below should prove useful in understanding what is going on with Larry and what direction should be taken to deal with the current problem.

A working copy of all activities can be found at
www.GrowingGreatRelationships.com

CHOICE THEORY CHART

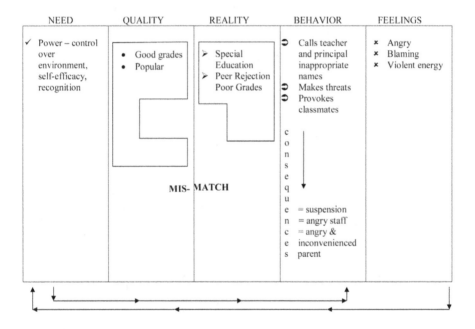

NEED	QUALITY	REALITY	BEHAVIOR	FEELINGS
✓ Power – control over environment, self-efficacy, recognition	• Good grades • Popular	➤ Special Education ➤ Peer Rejection Poor Grades	⊃ Calls teacher and principal inappropriate names ⊃ Makes threats ⊃ Provokes classmates	✗ Angry ✗ Blaming ✗ Violent energy
		MIS- MATCH	consequences ↓ = suspension = angry staff = angry & inconvenienced parent	

Let us first focus on the "Behavior" column. Inappropriate language, provoking classmates and verbal threats are the behaviors indicated. The consequences are a school suspension and the anger of the school staff and his mother. The next question to ask is, "What need was Larry meeting with the behavior?" Our needs theory tells us that behavior is purposeful and one's best attempt to meet a need at that moment. On the surface everything that happened to Larry appears negative and couldn't possibly be need fulfilling. However, if we look at the consequences of his behavior from a benefit perspective another picture emerges. A teacher, the assistant principal and his mother were all compelled to take action as a result of his behavior. He disrupted school routines and interrupted his mother's work. Adults in authority expressed anger towards Larry both in the tone of their voices and with their body language. We now need to go to the first column to understand what need Larry was attempting to meet with this behavior. Three adults had their need to feel in control impacted in a negative way. Disrupting their routines, evident in their anger, gives Larry the message that he has controlled his environment. By our definition, Larry has gained **power** through his inappropriate behaviors. Moving to the last column, we see that the feelings which Larry is experiencing are negative even though seemingly need fulfilling. Therefore, it is safe to conclude that the need will not be truly met and that this type of behavior will be repeated unless we break the cycle. The arrows on the bottom of the chart illustrate this. The need leads to the behavior. The feelings that follow the behavior are negative because despite Larry's temporary experience of increased power, his self-esteem will remain diminished because of the negative messages he is receiving. Furthermore, his need for love and belonging will also suffer as a result of parental disapproval.

The Quality World and Reality columns are useful in determining how to respond to Larry. Larry's quality or ideal world picture for feeling powerful in the school setting is hardly unusual. Like most children he wants good grades and social acceptance. However, we can see that his reality—poor grades, the label of being a special ed and peer rejection—have created a lack of congruency or mismatch between his quality world and his reality. Consequently, he has chosen a new set of behaviors to meet his need for power because following the rules has simply not worked.

Two approaches are required to help Larry. First we must assist Larry in making behavioral choices which meet his need for power but do not bring negative consequences. In addition, Larry needs to be coached to understand and re-configure his quality world image of being powerful. In the coming chapters we will discuss in greater detail how this can be accomplished.

Choice Theory teaches that the only behavior we can control is our own. Accepting that only you can control your behavior, rather than blaming someone else for what you do is the most difficult Choice Theory lesson to learn. In order for parents to assist their children in understanding that their behavior is purposeful, need fulfilling and within their control, they must be attuned to their own needs and the behaviors they have chosen to meet them. To help, let us re-visit the basic needs and offer some additional examples of how these needs play out in adulthood, especially in the context of family life.

Basic Needs

Love & Belonging—The need for unconditional acceptance and caring of spouse and children.

Power—The need to be a capable parent, to be effective in the eyes of our spouse, our family and community in child rearing.

Freedom—The need for a parent to recognize the necessity of some time off from the responsibilities of parenting to achieve individual freedom; it should be experienced without guilt because it restores our energy to parent.

Fun—An adult should be free to engage in playful behavior with a child that can be expressed in an adult world; play/fun should be a goal of the whole family not just the children.

Survival—The need to feel that life's fundamental necessities are being provided.

ACTIVITY # 1-4— *Fill in the blanks in the following exercise concerning your own needs as a parent.*

A working copy of all activities can be found at
www.GrowingGreatRelationships.com

I. Love and Belonging

A. Who gives me unconditional acceptance?

_____   _____

B. Who gave me unconditional acceptance as a child?

_____   _____

C. Am I my own best friend? Do I accept myself? Am I non-judgmental and believe that I'm doing my best? (Rank yourself from 1 to 10 as your own best friend.) _____

D. In the last week think about and write down five positive things you can say about yourself as a parent. (e.g. I took Barry to his soccer game and cheered. I asked Sara how she did on her biology quiz. I took a parenting book out of the library.)

_____

_____

_____

_____

_____

_____

E. Write down two things that you could do to take care of yourself this week.

_____

_____

II. **Power and Capability As A Parent.**

A. How do you rate as a capable parent from 1 to 10. A score of 5 is barely adequate.

1. I rate myself _____

2. My spouse/partner would likely rate me _____

3. My parents would likely rate me _____

4. My in-laws would likely rate me _____

5. My children's school would likely rate me _____

6. My friends would likely rate me_____

B. List at least two things that you <u>do</u> for yourself that don't take too much time. Also, list two things that you might want to <u>add</u> to your daily life. (HINT—keep it simple!)

DO (example: gardening)　　　ADD (example: power walk)

_____　　　_____

_____　　　_____

C. List at least two <u>skills</u> you use regularly and two things you used to do to feel important but don't do anymore.

SKILL　　　　　　　　　USED TO DO

(example: carpentry)　　　(example: coach sports)

_____　　　_____

_____　　　_____

D. Do you feel you are in a power struggle with someone? (If yes, with whom?)

YES _____ NO _____

III. **FREEDOM** (*Consider feelings such as anger, fear, strength, weakness, love, hate, depression, sensual, illness, hurt, dislike for family members*)

A. In my family I was discouraged from expressing feelings of _____

_____

I was allowed to express feelings of _____

B. I discourage my children from expressing feelings of _____

_____

I allow them to express feelings of _____

_____

C. I feel that I am meeting my freedom need. (rate 1 to 10) ____

D. List three responsibilities that curtail your freedom.

1. _____

2. _____

3. _____

Can any of these be shared? #1 ____ #2____ #3 ____

Can help be hired or traded? #1 ____ #2 ____ #3 ____

4. I might have more freedom as a parent if I felt less responsible for:

_____

5. I might have more freedom if I gave myself permission to:

_____

6. I might get more of what I want if I changed my quality world picture of: _____

_____

IV. FUN

A. List four fun things you can do for yourself that do not cost money:

   _____   _____

   _____   _____

B. When did you have fun with your child creating something?

   _____

C. Give an example of a behavior you might exhibit with a child but not

   with adults: _____

   _____

As a result of this exercise you have hopefully come to a greater understanding of how needs theory applies to your life, particularly as a parent. With this knowledge, you will be in a better position to help your children connect their behavior with satisfying a basic need. Their understanding of this crucial link is fundamental for implementing Choice Theory and maximizing responsible behavior.

What will follow is the combining of the principles of Theory Y leadership with a Choice Theory understanding of human behavior into a coherent blueprint for families. Grounded in a belief that it is possible for people to conduct themselves in a responsible and humane manner without the use of coercive punishments and coupling that belief with a understanding of how basic human needs drive behavioral choices we can embark on our parenting approach which we shall call **Family Centered Parenting**® (FCP).

Before we move on to the implementation phase of Family Centered Parenting with our children, the importance of creating a warm trusting relationship must again be strongly emphasized. Many of the strategies that will be explored depend on trusting relationships within the family. These can only be developed through the use of communication skills which reinforce the Theory Y principles of respect for the worth and dignity of the individual. Learning and practicing effective communication skills will enable us to model what we want our children to learn and allow us to coach them along the way.

Chapter 2

BE HEARD, BE LISTENED TO, BE UNDERSTOOD: PRINCIPLES OF EFFECTIVE COMMUNICATION

Effective communication is an essential building block of Family Centered Parenting. The proper use of communication techniques is the gateway to implementing every step of the process. Holding relationship building family meetings, creating mission statements and rules, solving problems and simply navigating our way through the daily routines of our lives requires us to communicate in a way that is need fulfilling for all. However, like all skills, we are not born with the ability to communicate effectively. We learn through imitation and trial and error experimentation and, over time, develop patterns of communication which vary in effectiveness from individual to individual. Therefore, as parent-models we need to be sure that we are teaching and demonstrating communication practices that will serve to enhance our children's ability to be successful in all aspects of their lives.

Seven rules of communication, along with practice activities, have been prepared to help break down the complexity of effective communication.

RULE #1— *Seek to understand before being understood.*

This rule is taken from Stephen Covey's, *7 Habits of Highly Effective People.* Mr. Covey calls it habit five. For work with families it should be considered as number one because, when not practiced, it virtually shuts down the negotiating and problem solving processes as well as interfering with any communication other than a direct command. There are several reasons why practicing seeking to understand before being understood is so powerful as a communications technique. The first, and the most basic, is that by checking for understanding we minimize miscommunication. Often disagreements can be traced to the simple fact that individuals did not correctly interpret the meaning that the other individual meant to convey. Second, if we refer back to our basic needs theory, we are reminded that being listened to and being recognized are ways of meeting one's need for power. By applying Rule #1 we guarantee that the person we are communicating with is being accurately listened to and thereby recognized as an individual worthy of being understood. This empowers the speaker, boosting their self-worth and making them far less likely to seek power through oppositional behaviors such as verbal or physical acting out. Third, when someone is given the opportunity to speak freely without being contradicted before they have completed their thoughts, they will be meeting another basic need—freedom. One means of meeting one's need for freedom is to feel free to express oneself.

The rule is easier to explain than to practice. Simply put, it means that we should keep quiet until the other person is finished talking. Actually, it is a little more complicated since understanding does not necessarily come from just allowing another person to speak. Active listening is a means to achieve the goal of understanding the other individual's point of view. Therefore, understanding is a product of active listening. The first step in active listening is not to interrupt the other person. The only exception would be to ask the other person to speak more slowly or more loudly if we are unable to comprehend their words. This is called hearing. It is more of a mechanical than a processing event and is a prerequisite to listening. Often, we don't interrupt but are merely biting our tongues while we await the moment to jump in with our point of view. If we focus on formulating a response instead of listening we are interfering with the process of understanding since our brains are not paying attention to the meaning the other person is attempting to convey.

Hearing coupled with full attention is active listening. However, this is still not understanding. The only way we can determine if we "got" the other person's point of view is by re-stating in our own words what we think the other person was trying to communicate and checking with them to see if we got it right. If the person agrees that we got it right then understanding has occurred and they are now ready to receive and hopefully understand our point of view. If the person says that we didn't get it, then we ask them to repeat the part or parts we didn't understand. We then repeat the process until the other person can verify that we got it.

It should be underscored that understanding is not synonymous with agreement. Just because you thoroughly understand another person you still have the right to disagree and present your point of view. What empowers the other person is the respect shown by you in being a listener in the full sense of the word. However, it is fair to expect the individual to spend as much effort in understanding you as you expended in attempting to understand them. Furthermore, if both parties follow the first rule, then it really doesn't matter which person goes first, since seeking to understand is the primary objective for both of you.

Now that the rule is understood, the next challenge is to become proficient in its practice. What follows are several steps to take to assist in refining your skills in understanding before being understood:

ACTIVITY # 2-1—

A working copy of all activities can be found at

www.GrowingGreatRelationships.com

---

1. The next time you have a conversation of some length, note how many times you interrupt the other person. Do not stop yourself but do make a mental note of the number times you interrupt in the time of the conversation.

2. Ask your spouse or a friend to help you. Tell him/her that you are practicing a new communication skill but do not say specifically what it is. Pick a topic with obvious sharply contrasting points of view (pro-life vs. pro-choice, for and against the death penalty, for and against the legalization of marijuana, tax cuts or deficit reduction, Red Sox vs. Yankees, Jerry Springer or Oprah, etc.). Ask your partner to choose the side of the issue that s/he is most comfortable with and invite him/her to begin the conversation. Your job is to persuade your partner that s/he is wrong. Remember that you might be role playing since you are taking the position opposite of your partner's regardless of your own point of view. React to your partner instinctively. Interrupt when you

feel s/he is mistaken and allow the emotional heat to rise if you begin to argue. After 10 minutes stop the process and ask your partner to tell you how s/he feel experienced the conversation. Specifically, ask them if they started to get angry and ask them why?

3. Repeat the exercise in number two, preferably not immediately afterwards, with the following changes. Be mindful that your purpose has not changed since you are still trying to change the other person's point of view.

   A. Do not interrupt your partner regardless of what you are feeling.

   B. When your partner appears to be finished (a long pause is a cue) ask him/her if s/he is complete for now.

   C. Say, "This is what I think I heard you say." Paraphrase what you believe were the main points of your partner's argument.

   D. Ask your partner if you got his/her points essentially correct. If not, ask him/her to repeat what you missed and repeat "C" until your partner says you got it.

   E. Briefly state your opinion on the subject.

   F. Ask your partner how s/he felt about the experience.

4. Compare your partner's reaction to the two exercises.

5. Write down in your organizer, put an index card on your refrigerator, write on your calendar or write down on any other place that catches your eye on a regular basis the following:

SEEK TO UNDERSTAND BEFORE BEING UNDERSTOOD by not interrupting and by stating and asking, "This is what I think I heard, did I get it right?"

RULE #2— *Validate, (give value to), the feelings of the other person even if you think they are wrong or exaggerated.*

Rule two provides us with a means of enhancing our understanding of verbal and non-verbal communication and a gateway to building relationships. Experiencing the totality of what someone is trying to communicate goes beyond comprehending the meaning of words. One needs to appreciate the emotional messages which shape the verbalizations and body language of the person we are dealing with in order to create and maintain the trust necessary for a productive relationship. Validating the feelings of another gives that person all-important and power-enhancing recognition. The validated individual feels that s/he has been truly listened to and understood.

ACTIVITY # 2-2— *Remember the last time you had either a terrible day or received some information that could have had a substantially negative impact on your life. If you called someone or sought someone out to speak to face to face, answer the following questions. If you didn't connect with the person you wanted, imagine what might have happened if you had reached them.*

A working copy of all activities can be found at
www.GrowingGreatRelationships.com

---

1. Why was this the person you chose to call?

2. What past experiences (if any) with this person contributed to your choice?

3. How did the person respond to your tale of what was going on in your life?

4. What did they say or do that made you feel better?

5. What did they say or do that was not helpful?

6. Think of a friend, relative or acquaintance that you would never call in this type of situation. Why wouldn't you?

7. Have you ever received a call or been invited to talk personally with someone who was in need (as described in this activity)?

8. Did you feel you helped the person who sought you out?

9. What did you say or do that made them feel better?

10. What did you say or do that was not helpful?

Experience shows that after our interaction with the person we chose to call we probably felt better. Interestingly, most likely nothing fundamentally changed in the conditions that prompted the call in the first place. However, if we reflect upon our own motivation we discover that the call was not intended to fix the problem(s). We were seeking support for our feelings. In fact, if we had been asking for some specific help solving our problem, we would not be able to hear it unless emotional support was given before advice was given. It is also highly likely that the individual named in response to question six was a person who is quick to offer solutions and suggestions. An advice giver is not necessarily a validator.

The key to validation, therefore, is to focus on the emotional state of the individual and acknowledge that that state is legitimate for them. Depending on the situation, problem solving might occur, but you won't get there until the person experiences emotional acceptance. Sometimes this can be difficult when we feel that the individual needing validation is responding in what we judge to be an inappropriate or exaggerated manner. However, it is imperative that we recognize that for that individual at that moment their emotional reaction is authentic and requires validation. Remember, we can validate without having to agree. This preserves the integrity of the relationship and keeps us from patronizing the individual in need.

A good example is responding to a crying child. Let us suppose that a 6-year-old was building a house with her Lego set. She accidentally slips and knocks down her project. She starts to cry and comes running to mom screaming, "Mommy, Mommy, I broke my special house." A common parental reaction, after assessing that the situation was not all that serious, is to quickly attempt to mollify the child by saying, "No need to cry, you can build another one." After all, by mom's standards, a collapsed Lego house is not a traumatic event. There was nothing inherently cruel or malicious in this response. Yet, this answer will not stop the tears nor will the proposed solution be heard. Instead, if mom's response was, "You sound really upset because your special house got knocked down," we would probably get a very different reaction from the child. In the second version, mom chooses words which validates her daughter's feelings. She acknowledged that her daughter was upset and that which actually occurred had triggered the tears. Notice that mom did not necessarily agree with her daughter's reaction but she used language that respected her child's emotional state. Furthermore, if she followed her validating statement with, "What can we do about it?" She would have made a smooth transition to problem solving. Again, successful problem solving follows the validation. Furthermore, by utilizing the phrase, "What can we do about it?" we invite the child to participate in the problem solving process.

Sometimes, as parents, we need to engage in proactive (preventative) validating. This means that we need to be attentive to our children's behavior and validate a significant change from either normal behavior or non-verbal communications of discomfort before our child specifically seeks out our attention. Taking action before something inappropriate occurs or before we are specifically asked makes the intervention proactive.

For illustration, imagine a 14-year-old boy, Ralph, sitting at the dinner table sitting quietly not making eye contact with anyone in the family. Ralph is usually a high-energy young man who has to be reminded to keep his voice down and not to tease his younger sister. Therefore, what we are observing is a child who, although not obviously calling attention to himself, is acting in a manner which is uncharacteristic or abnormal for him.

Ralph's parents have several choices. Let us assume that Ralph's behavior at the dinner table is linked to a rejection by a group of kids at school. He was invited by a friend to sit at a lunch table with several boys and girls who are thought to be the "in" group at school. One girl said to another, loud enough for Ralph to hear, "Who invited this geek to sit with us?" The other kids at the table started to giggle and Ralph's friend did not defend him. Ralph felt betrayed and rejected. This mood lasted through the afternoon and at the dinner table.

One approach would be to ignore him and be grateful that he is quiet for a change. The assumption being, that if he was really in trouble you would eventually find out. Another perspective is that Ralph is entitled to be in a bad mood and if he wants to talk about what's bothering him he knows where to find you. There are several reasons why these responses are inadequate. First, we really do not want to send Ralph a message that he needs to act out in order to get our attention. Clearly he is sending a non-verbal message that something is bothering him and that for reasons not known at the moment he has chosen not to verbalize what he is experiencing to his family. The risk of non-intervention is that he will not properly work through his issue. As a parent we need not only to be aware of our child's temperament in order to judge abnormal behavior but also our child's stage of development. An adolescent, like Ralph, is at a place where the importance of social acceptance by his peer group is particularly important. Adolescent children start to form their own identity by distancing themselves from their parents. This need to separate will often result in a child holding back information that they previously would have shared with the family. Therefore, it is especially critical in the adolescent years not to ignore a child's non-verbal manifestations of upset or confusion.

In the current example, the desired response from the parent to Ralph would be an observation such as, "Ralph, you are awfully quiet this evening and I see a sad look on your face, what happened to make you feel this way?" There is no guarantee that Ralph will respond, however, the validation of the observed behavior is an invitation for dialogue. In addition, it also provides the basis for further interventions if Ralph's behavior persists without explanation. If Ralph does reveal what happened in school, his parents must make sure to validate his sense of rejection before suggesting a remedy.

As adults we need to be especially mindful not to trivialize the feelings of our children in our zeal to soothe their pain. Our acquired wisdom has hopefully given us the perspective to deal with many of life's disappointments. Our children need to learn these coping skills by experiencing setbacks and bouncing back. The term resiliency is used in the counseling literature to describe this trait. The first step in developing resiliency is to acknowledge hurt feelings as being legitimate before assisting the child in problem solving. If we either attempt to soothe hurts by minimizing their impact or if we dictate solutions without sufficient work by our children we are shortchanging the learning necessary to develop resiliency.

ACTIVITY #2-3— FOR *each statement or observation, prepare a validating statement that you might make in response to the expressed or observed feeling:*

A working copy of all activities can be found at
www.GrowingGreatRelationships.com

---

1. Your six-year-old son comes over to you on the playground bench crying. He says that his friend played with his favorite truck and bent a wheel.

2. You just picked up your 15-year-old daughter after soccer practice. She barely says hello and is unusually silent on the way home.

3. You pass by your 14-year-old daughter's room. You hear her slam down the telephone and start crying.

4. Your 12-year-old son shows you his report card and starts cursing at his math teacher for giving him a C- for the marking period. He insists that he is being picked on by the teacher.

5. At dinner, you ask your 11-year-old how was his day. He gets agitated and recites all the things that went wrong and complains about his evening piano lesson interfering with all the homework he has to do.

Although there are no absolute right answers or prepared scripts to follow, some suggested responses with explanations will be offered for each situation:

Number one requires simple validation such as, "You sound upset, your favorite truck has a bent wheel. What can we do about it?" The caution here is not to minimize the child's emotional state. In his world the bent wheel is a big deal.

Number two is an example of a non-verbal signal of distress. "You seem awfully quiet, what's going on?" would be appropriate. This might or might not be enough. If she says, "nothing" you have a decision to make whether or not to pursue it. Trust your instincts and respond with, "Did something happen to upset you at practice?" If she still refuses offer your availability to talk when she is ready and remain attentive. Remember that proactive validation is really being sensitive to your child's moods. A parent should be the best judge of a child's emotional state. Respect you intuition and err on the side of intervening in an attempt to validate what you are observing. You are not telling your child how s/he feels. You are conveying how their behavior appears to you. This is an important difference and keeps a parent from becoming overly intrusive and presumptive of their child's feelings. The message that you are sending is that how they feel is legitimate, recognizable and that you are accessible to listen and problem solve if needed.

Number three does pose a real dilemma for a parent since the emotional state, crying behind a closed door, is not being displayed in an overt manner. The question then becomes whether or not the parent has sufficient grounds to intervene. Several factors should be weighed before a decision to act is made. First, we must assess the behavior in the context of the temperament and style of the child. As indicated earlier, proactive validation is based on a change in behavior from the norm for that child. If the young lady in this example is prone to volatile emotional responses then we might view the current situation as typical and not worth the potential violation of the teenager's privacy. However, if she is relatively stable and not prone to emotional outbursts then intervention is necessary. How we intervene is important. One possibility would be a knock on her door and a statement such as, "You sound angry and upset. I'm available now or after dinner to talk about it." This statement validates the feelings and offers specific options for follow up.

Those readers currently parenting teenagers might be anticipating that their invitation could be met with a distancing or overtly hostile reaction. It would certainly not be unexpected for the young lady in question to tell her parent anything ranging from, "There is nothing wrong," to "Leave me alone," or "It is none of your business." It is recommended that at this point parents should indicate that they care about how their child feels and that crying, yelling or other volatile emotional responses are usually indicators of distress and that you are merely responding in a caring way to this distress.

Number four is an overt declaration of a feeling state. In this case, it is clear to the parent that the child is focusing on blaming rather than taking responsibility for his behavior. In this situation it is crucial to validate the feeling before getting into the underlying issues. Remember, validation does not mean approval of the feeling. A suggested response might sound like. "You sound really angry about your report card grade and it seems that you think your teacher is to blame. What's going on?" As the story unfolds, utilize rule one and make sure you understand your child's point of view before giving your own. Validating and understanding will open the door for honest dialogue and problem solving between parent and child. The recognition a child gains by being truly heard and understood both rationally and emotionally is highly empowering. The result is that your child will learn that sharing with parents feels good and will become part of his/her repertoire of behaviors. It is also empowering for a parent to know that your child will come to you when stressed and view you as an essential resource in his/her life.

Number five poses a problem because of our tendency to fix what is wrong. Again, we must control our impulse to jump right in instead of validating the underlying emotional issue. A possible response, after the child has finished his litany of things going wrong, would simply be, "Sounds like you had a tough day." Again, no judgments or suggestions, just a validation of the stressful nature of what you are hearing and observing. A follow up question might be, "Is there anything I can do to help?" This will open the door if a problem solving discussion is needed for the situation. Validating in this situation serves to reinforce the competency and thereby the self-worth of your child. By responding in this manner, you are assuming that your child was able to navigate his way through a tough day. This builds his confidence and is consequently extremely empowering.

It is obvious from the five posed situations that how parents actually use language to validate is extremely important. The fine line between intrusiveness and involvement can best be drawn by the way we phrase our questions. To illustrate, consider the response to a child who is sulking. A typical parent reaction might be a question such as, "What's the matter with you?" If the tone is not one of annoyance, it could be viewed as a legitimate inquiry. However, it is too open-ended and does not validate the observed feeling. Children will frequently experience this type of question as if their space was being violated and respond with a, "None of your business," or "Nothing is wrong." Consider an alternative question, "You have a sad look on your face. Would you like to talk about how you are feeling?" The differences appear subtle but are significant. By putting into words what we are seeing—the sad face—we validate the feeling and send a clear message that we care. The "What is the matter?" type question could be received, even if we don't mean it, as if there is something wrong with being sad. This leads to denial and a distancing response from the child. In general, children, especially as they enter the adolescent years, experience ambivalence about sharing what is going on in their lives. On the one hand they are still seeking our parental approval and advice, while at the same time they are striving for independence and the support of their peers. The open-ended question makes it too easy to push parents away. Asking, "How was school today?" lends itself to the one word response "fine." On the other hand a more focused statement like, "Tell me about your day," invites conversation and opens the door for sharing in a non-judgmental atmosphere. This empowers the child because s/he is being heard and also empowers the parent by enhancing involvement in the child's world.

RULE #3— *Focus on the behavior not the individual.*

This rule deals with the importance of being attentive to how we use language. The intention of effective communication is to build and enhance relationships. As parents we are often placed in a role of enforcing limits and providing positive and negative feedback to our children. Frankly, no one really appreciates criticism even when it is couched in the euphemistic mode of "constructive criticism." Criticism touches our sense of self-efficacy, which is a component of our need for power. People, therefore, tend to process criticism as diminishing one's personal value. However, receiving feedback is a necessary part of learning. Behaviors and skills are learned and perfected through constant feedback as to how we are doing. The dilemma lies in providing feedback without it being received as criticism.

As parents we can do this by being mindful of how we choose our words when giving feedback. Using descriptive rather than judgmental language is the key.

For illustration let us take the case of Roger, a nine-year-old fourth grader. Roger's teacher called and left a message on the answering machine that Roger didn't turn in his homework. Roger's mother returns from work and listens to the message. She confronts him and says, "You are a liar. You told me last night that you finished your homework." Roger responds that he did do it but he left it on the bus. Mom then says, "You are a careless boy. What am I going to do with you? No TV tonight. Maybe that will make you more mindful of your responsibilities."

Some might argue that Roger's mother merely provided feedback given the circumstances. At first it appeared that he didn't tell the truth about doing his homework. Not telling the truth is a lie and people who tell lies are liars. When he offered the excuse she again provided feedback by indicating that losing homework on the bus is a thoughtless act and that he was, therefore, a careless boy. The problem with this method of feedback delivery is twofold. First, and most significant, we are labeling Roger not his behavior. This is criticism and goes to the heart of our "personhood" or self-esteem. It belittles the individual and usually provokes a defensive response. When our personhood is attacked it is normal to respond defensively. After all, who wants to willingly accept the characterization that s/he is a liar or a careless person? In addition, when we are in a defensive mode we are so preoccupied with protecting ourselves that there is little time or energy left for problem solving. Second, Roger's mother does not go beyond the criticism. She punishes without engaging in problem solving that is designed to prevent a future recurrence.

Let's consider an alternative response. After receiving the telephone call, Roger's mother says, "Roger, I got a call from your teacher about homework. I am pretty sure you told me last night that you completed your homework. I don't understand." After Roger's reply about leaving the assignment on the bus, she follows with, "It sounds like you weren't careful with the paper. What can you do make sure it doesn't happen again?" Notice that in this variation Roger's mother did not rush to judgment before obtaining the facts. Her statement that she didn't understand opened the door to explore the obvious discrepancy in facts before labeling the child. After the admission of leaving the homework is made, the focus is on the specific behavior. He wasn't careful at the moment. It is not a global picture of carelessness. She then sets the stage for a problem solving discussion. Roger in the second scenario will be far more willing to accept responsibility for a single careless act rather than own the characterization of being a careless person. In general, we are far more receptive to feedback when it does not diminish our sense of self and reduce our power. It is easier to accept a mistake as a singular act needing correction. This is especially true when we are also invited to participate in the improvement process.

ACTIVITY # 2-4— *Restate the following using descriptive rather than judgmental language.*

A working copy of all activities can be found at
www.GrowingGreatRelationships.com

---

1. You are too lazy to get your work done.

   _____

2. Breaking the glass was careless (irresponsible).

   _____

3. You are too stubborn to listen to reason.

   _____

4. Why must you be so loud when you come into the house?

   _____

5. You were rude to your grandmother when we visited.

   _____

6. You don't follow rules; you are a very defiant child.

   _____

7. I can't believe that you can be so sloppy.

   _____

8. My only conclusion is that you have a mean streak a mile wide.

   _____

9. I wish you weren't so shy when your cousins visit us.

_____

Here are some suggested alternatives. Match them with your answers.

1. Are you having difficulty completing your assignment?

2. Is there anything that you could have done differently to prevent breaking the glass?

3. I am having a hard time making myself understood.

4. I have a hard time concentrating with this level of noise.

5. I think grandma felt hurt by the way you talked to her.

6. I don't understand why the rule was broken. Was it clear?

7. Can I help you work more neatly?

8. At times, what I hear from you sounds like you don't care.

9. Are you more comfortable when you are quiet around people you don't know very well?

These suggestions are not meant to be the definitive alternatives to judgmental language but a guide as to how focusing on behavior might sound. Several themes are hopefully apparent. One is an emphasis on problem solving rather than broad based generalizations. Remember that the point of giving feedback is to help an individual to learn and to improve without undue attention to mistakes or failures. In addition, whenever possible, a parent should offer assistance or guidance. Feedback is the first step to learning. We all also need specific skills to improve and we should make ourselves available to help our children develop their skills. The process itself is need satisfying for parent and child. A parent feels they are fulfilling their parental role by providing assistance and guidance while simultaneously they are strengthening their relationships with their child. Children also experience the relationship enhancement with their parents and, furthermore, learn to accept the fact that their parents might be a valuable resource for solving problems.

The second theme is the use of "I" statements. People are far more receptive when we approach a situation from our own perceptual framework. It leaves room to resolve discrepancies without getting into a "he said, she said" type argument. "I" statements also serve to give us the freedom to express our own needs. This serves to legitimize our concern for the current issue. In number four, we are telling our child that the noise level is interfering with our ability to concentrate. This mitigates arguments since we do not have to try to establish a noise level that is acceptable by some outside measure. We are relaying to our child that something must be resolved to meet parental and child needs surrounding the issue of making noise.

RULE #4— *Avoid words that deal with past behaviors or continuous actions.*

This is a rather straightforward rule with one important element. Avoid using the words **always** and **never** or their synonyms when attempting to identify a behavior or to offer feedback to a child. When we are responding to a situation it is essential to focus on the present and future not on what happened last time. The reasoning is similar to the discussion in rule three. Our emphasis is on having our children accept responsibility for their behavior without diminishing their self-worth. When we refer to a behavior as a continuous act we again attack personhood. It is then natural for the individual to defend him/herself instead of taking responsibility for the behavior. By stressing the present we narrow our attention to a single event making it easier for the individual to own the behavior and commit to a plan for change.

Let us use Susan as an example:

Susan is an 11year old who seems to need a great deal of help in waking up and getting herself prepared to go to school in the morning. Susan's mother, Carol, frequently knocks at her door and reminds her that she has to get up. Several other times during the get ready routine Carol reminds Susan to hurry up or she will miss the school bus. One morning Carol, feeling particularly stressed, decides that she has had enough of Susan's procrastination and delivers the following message. "Susan, you never get ready on time and I always have to nag you to hurry up or you will miss your bus. I'm tired of this nonsense, you have to do something to change this behavior." Susan answers with. "That's not   true, the day before last I was up and around before you and last week when you had to leave early for work, I got up on time and made the bus even though you weren't home." Carol says, "Last week when I went to work early I had your grandmother call you to wake you up." Susan replies, "I was up before grandma called."

What has happened here is that Susan has successfully deflected her mother's intervention by raising issues of fact. Their dialogue centers on more around **when** it happened rather than **why** it happens. Carol's use of "never" and "always" precipitates a defensive reaction. People do not want to own the fact that they continually do something wrong. This goes to right to the core of our self-image and leads to denial. As previously indicated, it is very difficult for people to accept that the picture they have of themselves is consistent with chronically messing up or failing.

Those few individuals who do live in a world of negative self-imagery will probably be less reactive to a characterization on never being right. Yet, they too, will not engage in behavioral change when criticized because being a failure is consistent with their internal picture. This translates into a scenario where the negative behavior, as perceived by others, becomes need fulfilling and difficult to change. With these individuals, the description of continuous behavior also leads to a short circuiting the problem solving process.

As an alternative, we must focus on the specific instance when a behavior is problematic and avoid any reference to it being a constant or a permanent characteristic of the person we are dealing with. Returning to Carol and her daughter for illustration should prove helpful. Carol says to Susan, "I knocked on your door to remind you to get up this morning. I also had to remind you to eat your breakfast more quickly so that you wouldn't be late for the school bus. I really don't think I should do this. What do you suggest we do about it? I know we don't have time now so how about having a discussion this evening after dinner? Several things have changed between this approach and the previous one. First, Carol is dealing only with the present behavior. Although this has probably been going on for some time it is not productive to deal with a behavior that she wasn't willing to confront on previous occasions. A child is not responsible nor should be criticized because a parent has allowed a behavior to continue without significant parental attempts to help the child modify that behavior. Second, Carol is phrasing the intervention as an "I" statement. She is communicating her reason for intervention from a personal perspective and, furthermore, is inviting Susan to join her in the process of problem solving.

One might ask, "What if the situation occurs again shouldn't a parent refer to the fact that this is a matter that has been previously discussed?" The answer relates to the way the problem was originally addressed. Successful problem resolution (chapter 4 will go into this in detail) includes a plan for change. Therefore, when a behavior is repeated we refer the child to The Plan and ask why it did not work.

We then ask the child to come up with a different plan since the first attempt wasn't successful. Obviously, the second and subsequent plans require more effort than the original plan. This method allows us to deal with misbehavior or rule breaking as a single event rather than a continuous act.

RULE #5— *Control your emotions when responding to your child.*

There are several reasons why this rule is so important. The first one is a parent's role as a model of acceptable behavior. Simply put, children do what we do not what we say. We are genetically programmed to be highly imitative. Therefore, our children learn by what they see far more than from what we tell them to do. If we lecture our children about controlling their temper and then they witness us indulging in an episode of road rage, it is certain that they will learn more from our behavior than our words. If we expect children to control their emotions and not to throw a temper tantrum or yell at their siblings we cannot in turn react to them in an emotionally volatile manner. If we confront a child in an agitated state, s/he will quickly respond with, "Why is it all right for you but not for me to raise my voice?" This is a legitimate inquiry and any explanation is really indefensible including a rather feeble one such as, " I can yell because I am the grownup." Therefore, simply put, we must practice what we preach.

Another reason for controlling our emotions is the paradoxing affect our out-of-control behavior has on some children. Children, who are not getting their power needs met, will view an adult's emotional outbursts as their way of controlling that adult. In its most severe manifestation, this pattern is known as "Oppositional Defiant Disorder." Basically, when one gets in this pattern you become a prime example of the **Myth of Control**, which states:

Arbitrary rules or authoritarian demands intended to exercise control are viewed as provocative and are seen as an invitation to act against those very rules or demands. Therefore, the exercise of control often results in a loss of controls.

In effect, our emotional outburst empowers a child. When a child, especially one who is particularly powerless, gets an adult in an authority position angry they are getting their needs met at a level sufficient enough for them to endure the negative consequences dispensed by the adult. Children quickly learn what pushes our buttons and will zoom right in on our vulnerabilities so that they can provoke the volatility that reinforces and perpetuates the very behavior that most upsets us. We often lose sight of the fact that children perceive adults as powerful figures who appear to be in control of their environments far more than they really are. Therefore, when these perceived powerful figures erupt because of what the child did, the child experiences a surge in his/her own sense of power.

In practice, our best defense against the trap of the myth of control is to be continually mindful of how parental outbursts empower our children in a negative way. In addition, we need to feel secure about our roles and ourselves. For example, if a parent feels that they are not spending enough time with their child, a child's hurtful accusation of not caring about them could easily lead to an angry response. If we experience hurt and guilt, we often will express it in the form of anger. The parental response, usually at a high decibel level, often goes like this. "How dare you say I don't care about you, look at all the things I do for you…………." At this point the child has become victorious. They have provoked their parent into an explosive and defensive posture.

The most effective responses to accusations from our children that we have let them down is to focus on the process not on the specific words used by the child. Instead of getting drawn into angry and defensive reactions, we must re-direct the conversation to the behavior that caused the confrontation in the first place.

For example, Sarah returns from work and sees that her 10-year-old son Josh has not cleaned up after his snack. There is an established family rule regarding this chore so there is no ambiguity about Sarah's intervention. She says to Josh, "What happened? There is a mess on the table from your snack." Josh responds, "You are never here when I get home from school to pay attention to me." If this answer taps into feelings of guilt Sarah might have about being a working mom, she could easily fall into Josh's trap and get defensive and emotional. Josh not only goes after Sarah's sensitivity to not being home but he also baits her with the word never. Sarah could easily get angry and say, "How dare you say that? You know how I've changed my hours so that I can get home earlier on Tuesdays." Josh would probably come back with an additional accusation and before long the incident that caused the confrontation is forgotten as Sarah's attention turns to her own feelings and upset with her emotional outburst. Josh has learned to both deflect his mother's attention and to empower himself by provoking Sarah into a defensive and angry position.

Alternatively, Sarah might have responded to the original situation with, "There is a mess on the table from your snack. What is our rule about cleaning up?" Josh then attempts to deflect and provoke. Sarah responds, in a neutral tone of voice, with "Josh, the question I asked concerns our rule about cleaning up. What is your answer?" If Josh persists, Sarah re-directs attention to her question and then informs Josh that she will no longer engage in this conversation and that he is on shut-down (defined in the next chapter) until he is ready to answer her original question. Sarah, in this case, has not taken the bait. She is mindful of Josh's strategy and re-focuses on the issue at hand instead of rising to his challenge. Since Josh is no longer empowering himself by provoking Sarah emotionally, he will choose alternative behaviors to feel powerful which are more appropriate and positively need fulfilling.

Another important reason for controlling our emotions is the nature of our decision-making ability when we are angry. Researchers have been able to measure the changes in brain chemistry when we are experiencing highly charged emotions. When we are angry our adrenaline surges and places our body in what is known as a "fight" or "flight" mode. This state is characterized by increased blood flow to the muscles and sensory apparatus needed to run for our lives or to do defend ourselves from physical harm. However, at the same time it virtually shuts down the higher level thinking and analytical parts of our brain. This phenomenon is called "downshifting" by neuro-physiologists. Although an adaptive mechanism under certain circumstances—it is not a good idea to ponder the relative muscle mass of a grizzly bear that is about to have us for lunch. Our physiology does not know the difference between responding to a sudden actual threat and the anger at a child that leads to yelling or at striking. Another example will resonate with anyone who has ever prepared for a test and then totally blanked during the test only to recall, after the test, everything they studied. This phenomenon, known as test anxiety, clearly illustrates what happens to our brains when we shift into the fight or flight mode. This particular area of research is also helpful in understanding why so many people are suffering from stress related medical disorders. The stresses of our modern culture inappropriately triggers the fight or flight response that has evolved over millions of years in a far different environment. What was once a survival mechanism for our ancestral hunters and gatherers is physically debilitating for human beings in the 21st Century.

In essence it means that we don't think really well when we are angry or highly agitated. The capacity for creative solutions, so needed by parents, is greatly diminished when we are angry and leads to responses for which we are ashamed of or that are so over-reactive that we have to beat a less then graceful retreat from our own declarations.

An illustration should clarify:

After a particularly long and stressful day, David's dad, Mark, arrives home and starts to look through the mail. Because he has a pet peeve about skyrocketing telephone costs he opens the cell phone bill first. The extra minute charges for his 15-year-old's cell phone are $97.00 for the month. He warned David last month to curb his cell phone use and David assured him he would. Mark starts to boil and yells upstairs for David to come down. Of course, David is on his cell and doesn't hear his father. This gets Mark even more annoyed and he dashes up the steps to David's room. He is now at full boil. He pushes open David's door and demands that he get off the phone. David is talking to his girlfriend and gets embarrassed. He yells back at his Dad to get out of the room. Mark yanks the phone out of David's hand and tells David he has lost his phone privileges for two months. He storms out of the room with David accusing him of being unfair. Later that evening, after dinner and some quiet time, Mark realizes that his own behavior was irrational. He acted in a manner contrary to what he has preached to his children as appropriate. Furthermore, he realizes that David depends on his cell to communicate with his study group which he needs to complete many of his homework assignments. David is also part of a community service project that utilizes his cell as a hotline for teens that need to talk to a peer. Mark must make some concessions but he doesn't want to back down from his punishment.

This is a clear example of anger getting in the way of good parental decision making. Once Mark's brain downshifted he was unable to remember and utilize the principles of effective communication. What could Mark have done differently? The fact that he had a stressful day and that he hates telephone bills is not in our area of analysis. However, Mark needed to be mindful of his own hot buttons before he challenged his son. Our best defense against triggering the fight or flight response is to be aware of what sets us off. Mark knows about his telephone bill hang up and might have decided that it was not a good time to open that bill. Even if he did, when the anger started to rise, Mark needed to remind himself that avoiding a discussion with David was necessary until after he calmed down. If he would have let David know that he needed some time to talk to him and calmly approached him with the bill and a question such as, "I'm really concerned with the bill for your cell phone. What are we going to do about it?" the chances of David taking responsibility and entering into a plan with his father for dealing with the issue would have been greatly increased. Sometimes we just have to say to our children, "I'm too angry to discuss this with you right now. I need to cool off before we process what happened." Conversely, children who have downshifted also need to be told that they should cool off before you will deal with their issues.

RULE #6— Be mindful of your non-verbal communications.

This rule logically follows the previous rule because at times we might think we are controlling our anger through a careful choice of words but in reality we are sending a very different message to the listener. Non-verbal communications deals with the process of communication that isn't based in language. Also called "paraverbals" it refers to our body language, personal space, the volume of our voices and the speed or cadence of our speech.

Much has been written about the subtleties of body language, including facial expressions, as a conveyance of meaning. For sake of simplicity we are going to deal with only the most obvious and easiest to control aspects of body language as they relate to communication with our children. One of the most important is posture.

If one is trying to create an atmosphere conducive to negotiations and problem solving, our body position must not send a message that makes the other person feel threatened. Our perceived threatening posture can trigger anxiety and a possible fight or flight response in our children. This will lead them to defensiveness and to downshifting their brains to a non-thinking level. The posture considered most aggressive is chest first. When we approach an individual and lean forward with our upper body we are sending a message of dominance which engenders submissiveness or anger/challenge. Neither state promotes dialogue and problem solving. Therefore, we should be mindful that although we do want to make eye contact, it is best to turn our upper bodies, shoulder aimed at the other person, when we are attempting to dial down the emotional level of a confrontation between a parent and child. Another posture of dominance is looking down at someone. When an individual must look up to speak s/he has been placed is a position of subservience. This is especially true when there is a great disparity in height as is often the case with a parent and a younger child or when one individual is standing while the other one is sitting. It is also a factor when an adult is standing near a child.

Another aspect of body language is personal space. Generally speaking people are most comfortable when the person they are dealing with is anywhere from 1.5 to 3 feet away from them. As a rule of thumb, one arm's length distance from another is usually the required zone of personal space. The space varies among cultures and is influenced by the nature of the relationship between individuals. We probably require less personal space with someone with whom we have a close personal relationship. However, when we do invade the personal space/comfort zone of an individual, they will experience a level of discomfort which could very well provoke the fight or fight response and hinder effective communication.

The paraverbals of voice volume and cadence of speech are worthy of exploration. When we raise our voice it is experienced as provocative by the listener and will lead to defensiveness or a full scale fight or flight response when we reach the level of yelling or screaming. Cadence, the speed of our verbalizations, is also significant. Again, when someone speaks to us very rapidly, we tend to experience a defensive feeling. Therefore, if someone is shouting at us and speaking rapidly, the two combined will generally put the listener into an agitated state.

In summary, our goal in communicating with our children is to help create the conditions for effective communication to occur. In order to accomplish this, the atmosphere must be as emotionally neutral as possible, especially when we are discussing an issue which in of itself is emotionally charged. Therefore, mindfulness of those non-verbal aspects of communication will help create a climate where we can deal with all of our creative and thoughtful abilities and not respond on a primitive fight or flight level.

ACTIVITY # 2-5— *In the course of dealings with acquaintances and colleagues over the next several days, attempt to do the opposite of what is recommended as appropriate non-verbal communications and note the reaction of the person you are interacting with. For example, deliberately invade personal space, speak louder and faster than normal and assume body positions, which have been mentioned as being provocative. As a cautionary note, do not do this when you yourself are feeling angry or upset and cease the behavior when you notice a reaction in the other party. It would be helpful to ask the individual you are experimenting on for feedback as to how they experienced you.*

A working copy of all activities can be found at
www.GrowingGreatRelationships.com

RULE #7—*Whenever possible, catch your child doing something right and offer words of validation or praise.*

This rule takes us beyond the previously discussed notion of validation. In Rule #2 we focused on validating feelings, verbal or non-verbal, when they were directed at us. Here we are talking about proactive validation. That is we will validate through language and physical gestures our child's behavior when the behavior affirms the family mission statement, is in accord with established rules, or demonstrates a high level of quality in the overall manner in which our child is conducting his/her life. The mechanisms for validation are words or non-verbal expressions of praise. There are several reasons why this is so important. To begin with, behavioral scientists have long known that behavior is shaped best by reward. In other words, human beings, like all animals, will tend to repeat a behavior that is followed by a pleasurable state that is created through reward. Therefore, in order to make sure that desirable behaviors continue we must be mindful of these behaviors. This is more difficult than we might realize. The old adage about the "squeaky wheel" certainly applies when it comes to how we deal with our children. We tend to be far more responsive to negative behaviors than the appropriate or outstanding ones. However, when our children experience the words of praise that follow certain behaviors they will then more likely repeat them. Furthermore, from a needs theory basis, praise or approval acknowledges the child thereby boosting his/her power needs. External validation can be an important pathway in enhancing self-worth and its potency shouldn't be underestimated.

In order for praise to be most effective it must be sincere, salient and delivered as close to the desirable behavior as possible. Sincere refers to authenticity on the part of the parent delivering the praise while saliency refers to its meaningfulness.

"Sweetheart, you put on such a nice outfit. You are going to be the prettiest girl in your class." This statement is clearly praising a behavior, picking out nice clothes, but the second part is clearly inauthentic and not terribly meaningful. The parent can't possibly know who is the prettiest girl in the class. This kind of "praise overkill" devalues the message and in the long run makes it harder for the child to believe any form of praise. Using descriptive language that is to the point conveys the praise message the best.

For example, your nine-year-old boy is introduced to a family friend who comes to the house. When introduced, he sticks out his hand and says, "Nice to meet you Mr. Simms." Somewhat startled by this rare moment of civility, a private comment to your child such as, "That was a nice greeting to Mr. Simms, I really appreciated it," would be a highly effective reinforcer. This praise statement is sincere, focused and not overly drawn. It can be easily accepted by the child and the demonstration of parental approval would serve to empower the child by raising his self worth.

Praise does not need to be elaborate. A "good job" is often a sufficient and effective praise statement when catching a child doing something right. A gesture such as a "thumbs up" or a smile and a pat on the back can be even more powerful than words in conveying acceptance and approval to a child. However, timing is important. Again, it should be emphasized that praise should be delivered as close to the event as possible. This increases the saliency and maximizes the effect of the reward of approval. That is why it is important to acknowledge the event in some fashion even if you have to postpone the explanation.

For example, you just picked up your 14-year-old daughter and her friend at the mall after an afternoon movie. Your daughter invites the friend over for dinner because her Mom is away on business and won't be home till late. You know that your daughter is giving up an invitation to a party in order to entertain her friend. If you praise her publicly it will cause embarrassment. This is the time for a quick smile or other private gesture. Later on, when the two of you are alone, you can offer the words of praise that are specific to the situation.

Another caution about praise statements is not to couple an utterance of praise with a criticism or suggestion. Sometimes in our strong desire to teach our children we might offer a statement such as, Good work but if you changed _____ it would be better." It is suggested that the praise statement stand on its own and feedback be provided in a separate interaction. Remember that we are attempting to build self-worth and do not want to contaminate or dilute parental approval with a suggestion that takes away from that very approval. This is confusing to a child and shakes their confidence.

For example, a parent reviewing a child's report card might easily say, "Great job, you got an "A" in reading. But your math slipped to a "B", what happened?" This type of praise robs the child of the feeling of success for his/her reading performance. An alternative might sound like, "Great job in reading. You should be really proud of yourself for the hard work you put it. Now let us look at your math grade." Although in the second example, reading and math grades were discussed close to together in time, the parental phrasing of the praise message uncoupled the reading from the math. This allowed the child to experience the full positive effect for his/her reading performance and yet still be accountable to discuss the situation with math.

One might reasonably ask, "Do I have to praise my child for everything they do right?" The answer is clearly "no." There are several reasons. First, the constant praise will appear inauthentic to the child. They don't expect to be praised for everything and if they are, they will view it as insincere or manipulative. Second, behavioral scientists have learned that behaviors persist longest when they are rewarded intermittently. Therefore, an occasional reward for more routine desired behaviors is most effective. Furthermore, the purpose of the rule is to catch your child doing something right. The assumption behind it is that this is a new behavior being praised. It is not ordinary and it is particularly worthy of your approval. Like all good things, too much can sometimes undermine your intended purpose. We do want to build our children's self-esteem for legitimate accomplishments without making them overly dependent on external approval. Remember our love and caring for our children should not be the reward. Demonstrating love is unconditional and should be totally disconnected from performance. Our children need to know they are loved and cared about even when their actions do not meet our approval.

We can accomplish this by being generous with our "I love you" messages and remember to offer them after an episode requiring a disciplinary intervention. Children, and adults for that matter, need to know that they are lovable and valuable individuals even when they make mistakes.

Chapter 3

WHERE IT ALL HAPPENS: THE FAMILY MEETING

The cornerstone of the Family Centered Parenting approach is the creation of a sacred family space, the family meeting. Structuring the meeting and institutionalizing it in the life of the family as a ritual is where we actually begin Family Centered Parenting. The family meeting can be thought of as the trunk of the Family Centered Parenting P.E.A.C.E. tree (See Summary). All of the parenting practices discussed grow out from the trunk like the branches of a tree. Continuing the tree analogy, the family meeting allows feedback to flow back from the end of the branches, where the family interacts with the outside world, to the meeting space, the trunk, where results can then be analyzed and used to either make changes or validate what is actually happening. This ensures that the parenting process remains an evolving and self-correcting system. To make this happen we will explore the why, when, and how of creating and maintaining family meetings.

The key word is ritual. All families have their own unique spoken and unspoken traditions and these serve to bind the family together. The family meeting must be established as an essential family ritual. Rituals, by definition, are practiced with a high degree of consistency and importance. Therefore, parents, as role models, are responsible for taking the leadership role in scheduling and explaining to the children the reasons for the family meeting. Parents are the primary force in creating the family meeting as a ritual because of their ability, through the scheduling process, to make meeting time a high priority in the life of the family. If done properly, meetings become highly need fulfilling, thereby providing positive experiences for all members of the family.

There are two types of meetings, the regular and the ad-hoc. The regular meeting should be held at least once a week and is oriented to family maintenance, proactive problem solving, and teaching/learning. Maintenance time is devoted to receiving feedback on how well family rules and practices are operating and to making needed adjustments. In addition, maintenance also serves as a good time for family members to report how things are going in their lives. With hectic family schedules and multiple individual activities it is important for family members to simply update each other. This kind of sharing not only meets the need for love and belonging but also fills the need for power by virtue of individual family members gaining recognition by being heard.

Proactive problem solving concerns the anticipation of a potential problem which a member of the family thinks will occur in the future and should be dealt with before the fact. One type of proactive problem solving is advance planning for a specific event. Examples include planning a family trip, behavioral expectations for an upcoming family reunion and preparing for the holiday season. The other type of proactive problem solving focuses on day to day routines. These include setting guidelines and rules for issues such as homework, bedtimes, sleeping at a friend's house, curfews, household chores, telephone usage, etc. The adult will most often initiate proactive discussions. However, over time children will begin to raise issues in advance because they too have learned that proactive attention reduces later conflict and provides more freedom in managing their lives. Boundaries based upon consistent and understandable rules provide children with a structured world which is predictable and secure. This helps children to meet their need for power, by promoting self awareness, and their need for freedom by establishing parameters within which they can then mange aspects of their own lives. Most importantly, the process itself also promotes the need for freedom by giving children input into the rules that govern their lives. Allowing them to express their wants and having those wants listened to by parents is fulfilling the need for both freedom and power. It should not be overlooked that this process, although more time consuming than an authoritarian approach, is also far more need fulfilling for parents. Parents too, in a proactive discussion, are able to voice to the children and to their partners what they need to feel in order to be empowered as parents. Parents begin to feel empowered and free when they are able to have a forum to state their expectations for how their children should behave and be reasonably assured that they will be heard.

The teaching/learning segment of the meeting provides an opportunity for the family to discuss a broader issue that might involve the acquisition or imparting of new information. Initiation of these activities is usually undertaken by the parent, yet as confidence increases over time children tend to take more of a leadership role. A good example of a teaching/learning meeting would be a discussion on drugs and alcohol. Utilizing the family meeting for talking about a "hot topic" serves to neutralize the awkwardness for parent and child. Most parents find sexuality and substance abuse as the two major hot topics. Parents often find it difficult to initiate conversations on hot topics because they are never certain when to start discussions. This results in just putting it off until a crisis erupts. Parents are often fearful that the children will perceive the raising of the issue as an accusation of misbehavior and/or they feel sufficiently insecure about the topic itself to discuss it. Having it on the agenda of a family meeting answers the timing question by making the topic appear to be relatively routine. Additionally, the meeting format tends to somewhat neutralize the embarrassment felt by parents when speaking about these issues because the meeting is not being called for the sole purpose of discussing a hot topic.

Let us take substance abuse as an example. Most experts working on substance abuse prevention indicate that children should begin to discuss drugs and alcohol with their parents before they are directly exposed to the hard choices about usage. Unfortunately, in our culture, this means raising the issue no later than fourth grade. There are many different ways to proceed. Choosing an approach should obviously depend on the age of the children. Therefore, a good beginning is to first find out how much information your children already have. Simply asking a child to share his/her thoughts on the subject with other family members is a good starting place for assessing prior knowledge and belief systems. A parent, at this stage, must take great care not to overreact to attitudes that are contrary to one's adult values. Certainly we want to make sure our children understand our values but we must do it in a way that doesn't feel like a morality lesson. The family meeting format provides the environment for open discussion permitting parents to make a case for their values without sounding like judges or moralists. In addition, the family meeting becomes a safe place for children to reveal their fears and insecurities that often accompany the "hot topic" issues. Besides hot topics, the teaching learning meeting is a good time to wrestle with issues concerning moral development and ethical behavior. "What if?" type questions are very useful in these discussions. For example, you might ask your child what she would do if she found a wallet in the street or what would you do if a friend told you he was going to do something dangerous but made you promise not to tell anyone else. These kinds of questions are highly stimulating yet, since they refer to hypothetical situations, are emotionally non-threatening. This permits the child to explore and question his/her core values and beliefs with the guidance of parents.

Ad-hoc meetings, by definition, should be called as needed. Each family must have its own rules to determine who can ask for an ad-hoc meeting. These meetings are usually geared towards the problem solving of a particular issue that is imminent and can't be put off until the next regular meeting or to dealing with an issue that is at a crisis level. It should be noted that ad-hoc meeting issues might not be resolved in one meeting and a follow-up meeting will need to be scheduled.

Family schedules should be coordinated so that all members of the family can guarantee a period of uninterrupted time for the regular meeting. The length of the meeting will vary with the agenda, the age of the children, and the communication styles of the family members. However, it is unusual to have a meeting for less than 30 minutes.

The initial step for the parents (parent in a single parent home) in creating the meeting ritual is to set the tone for the occasion. By announcing in advance to the family that a meeting will take place at a certain time and place in the home and that all members of the household are expected to attend, parents have marked the event as significant. For most families juggling schedules to find the time will prove a substantial undertaking. However, the complicated calendaring process in of itself will send a message that the meeting is truly serious business.

There are no strict guidelines as to the best time and place for a meeting. Some families will choose to hold them immediately after a family meal at the dining room table. Others might choose a weekend morning. The key is in making the effort to hold the meeting and to plan a back-up time if some unforeseen event causes a meeting to be canceled.

The initial meeting should have two goals. First, the reason for having a meeting must be communicated. This is not a shared decision because attendance is not an option for the children. Therefore, parents must be very clear in stating that the meeting is an attempt for all members of the family to work together to make their family a safe and special place. Parents should talk about their own needs to feel successful as parents and should also mention that the meeting format represents an opportunity for the children to have a forum for input into family decision making. Although these concepts will not entirely be grasped at the first meeting, and no doubt will be repeated many times especially with younger children, it is important to begin using the vocabulary of the Family Centered Parenting model.

The second major goal is to establish ground-rules for conducting the meeting. Children, along with the adults, should be invited to offer suggestions about appropriate guidelines for the conduct of a meeting. Issues that need to be resolved include; taking turns to speak, interruptions, defining rules for appropriate language, dealing with angry feelings, hurtful and judgmental comments, maintaining confidentiality and refusal to attend a meeting. While the family is mastering the meeting process it would be advisable for a parent to assume the role of leader. If the family chooses, over time this role can be assumed by other members of the family. Keep in mind throughout the meetings that the process on how decisions are reached are just as or even more important than the decisions themselves. There is no one best way to conduct a meeting, and furthermore, ground-rules should be subject to constant revision as the family becomes more expert in holding family meetings. However, as we recall from our Theory Y leadership principles, rules are far easier to enforce when those affected by rules have a role in formulating them. Therefore, we must be vigilant in seeing that all family members have input in setting meeting guidelines and that each family member commits to accepting a rule even if it is not his/her preferred option. Brainstorming is a suggested methodology for this type of discussion. Brainstorming is a well-established process for a group to help generate the broadest variety of ideas while ensuring maximum participation in decision making.

Let us look at how the brainstorming technique can be used to help a family create its meeting guidelines. First, the family needs to choose a facilitator whose role is to keep order and to record responses from the group. The next step is a re-statement of the main principle of brainstorming—which is that any idea offered by a participant is to be recorded without comment by the group or the facilitator. This is key to the success of the brainstorming process because offering immediate feedback of a negative nature tends to inhibit responses. Therefore, in the beginning of the brainstorming session, judgmental comments are put on hold until the list of alternatives is complete. The facilitator, with family input, should then establish a time limit for the idea portion of the brainstorming process. In the current example, the facilitator would then ask for suggestions as to ground-rules for holding a family meeting. As responses are given, the facilitator should record them on a surface that is visible to the whole family. When the group says enough, or time runs out, the next phase begins. Each idea on the list is then evaluated and a decision is reached on whether or not that idea is to remain.

It is strongly recommended that, if possible, decisions be reached by consensus. Consensus decisions are those where, after discussion, all participants are willing to say "O.K., I can live with it for now." This means that those who disagree must give their consent. Although time consuming, consensus decision making creates the most ownership on the part of the group. In families, ownership is so important that it is worth the extra time to attempt to reach a consensus. Majority decisions are less responsive to ownership and should be employed only when time is critical or a consensus cannot be achieved.

The brainstorming sequence concludes with a memorializing of the outcome. In the present case this would be an agreed upon list of ground-rules for family meetings. The list should be readily available and should be quickly reviewed before the beginning of each meeting. It should be noted that any ground-rule is subject to modification by the family after appropriate discussion and a consensus decision.

What Are We All About?
Our Family's Mission/Vision

Once the ground-rules are established and the family has had experience with the process of brainstorming, the next phase is the creation of a family mission/vision statement. Creating mission and vision statements have become standard operating procedure in most business and non-profit organizations. They are intended to focus all members of the enterprise on the fundamental beliefs of the organization and what it is trying to achieve. It is supposed to be a collaborative process where the work of creating the statement becomes almost as valuable as the end product itself.

The mission statement movement, like most managerial innovations, has gone through a cycle ranging from the panacea for solving all organizational problems to cliché. It is not uncommon to walk into the office of a company or agency and see the mission statement framed and hanging in a prominent place in the reception area. Whether or not the mission statement is truly reflective of the culture of the organization is largely defined by the degree of integrity that the process was conducted. Countless hours and dollars have been devoted by organizations in creating mission statements. Frequently, utilizing the expertise of management consultants, employees and managers have sat together in good faith and have created mission/vision statements for their organization only to find their work reduced to a quote in an annual report or newsletter and little else. Those enterprises where mission statements retain their value as guideposts to the true purpose of the organization understand that the mission statement must be a living and breathing document. The statement should be created through open discussion with consensus decision making. The discussion should reveal discrepancies among individuals which cannot be ignored. When disagreements about goals and values appear, they should become subjects for further exploration. This is how the process can spur growth and change. In addition, the mission statement must be re-visited, involve new employees as they join the workforce and be kept alive.

The mission statement process is particularly well suited for families. In his well respected book *The Seven Habits of Highly Effective Families,* author Stephen Covey calls the family mission statement "a vision of what we wanted our family to be like, what we would live by, what we would stand for—even die for. It would be a vision that was shared and owned by all family members, not just the two of us" (page 76). Keep in mind that the reason the mission statement works so well for families lies in its ability to be highly need fulfilling for all participants.

The process of developing a mission statement meets both the need for love and belonging and the need for power. Working together as a family to develop the statement is an experience which enhances personal relationships among family members. In addition, when completed, the statement serves to recognize the uniqueness of the family that prepared it. This creates the feeling of ownership shared by the contributing members of the family. The personal bond coupled with the knowledge that the mission statement is owned only by the family proves highly fulfilling of the need for love and belonging. When the mission statement is developed with the appropriate respect for each member of the family's point of view everyone's power, as defined by respect and being listened to, is also enhanced.

ACTIVITY # 3-1— *To assist the family in developing its mission statement, use the following guiding questions to focus discussion. The questions do not need to be answered at the first meeting. Family members should have some time to collect data and consider their answers.*

A working copy of all activities can be found at
www.GrowingGreatRelationships.com

1. What characteristics form an ideal family?
2. How close is our family to this ideal? Where do we meet it? Where are we deficient?
3. How do you think others see our family?
4. Have you ever been ashamed or embarrassed about any aspect of our family life? If yes, when and how?
5. What do we expect from our children? (PARENTS ONLY)
6. What do we expect from our parents? (CHILDREN ONLY)
7. What do we expect from our siblings? (CHILDREN WHEN APPLICABLE)
8. If a tragedy befell our family and we all died in a sudden accident, what would you like to have said about the family at a memorial service?

In Covey's book, he relates that his family took eight months to prepare their mission statement which was then framed and hung on their living room wall. Although laudable, it is not necessary to devote that much time to its preparation especially if younger children are involved. Furthermore, if we view the mission statement as a work in progress, we can live with an agreed upon or partial statement and modify it as new data is received and assimilated by the family in the course of the meeting process.

As an example, the author's family developed the following mission statement. This is not intended to be a model, simply one approach out of many possibilities. At the time it was developed the children were aged 14, 12 and 9.

"The mission for our family is to create and maintain a safe place where each member of the family feels loved for who they are without judgment. Treating each other with respect, honesty and consideration of his/her best interests as we each pursue our individual journeys is of greatest importance. Our home shall always be open to those in need and serve as relief from the pressures of everyday living."

Our mission statement evolved over a series of family meetings and was revised when our oldest child left for college. It was posted on the refrigerator and served as our permanent reminder of who we were and where we wanted to be. Often, at family meetings, the mission statement was brought to the table as a benchmark for making decisions. Any member of the family felt free to refer to and to hold him/herself or other member of the family accountable to our mission. In fact, this is the most valuable function of the mission statement. Not only does it serve as a roadmap to chart the course of family life, but it also allows members of the family to make a value judgment about their behavioral choices that is based on the mission, not on the subjective opinion of another individual. A family member becomes comfortable asking him/herself or another member of the family the question, "Is your choice (behavior) consistent with our family mission statement?" This is a very powerful intervention for several reasons. First, it focuses on the individual making choices. This is highly consistent with the basic principles of Choice Theory. Second, it reinforces the notion that the mission statement is a standard which articulates our quality world definition of reality against which we can compare the reality of our current behavioral choices. Lastly, the question reinforces the sense that the mission statement is "our mission statement." It belongs to only our family. This serves to further strengthen ownership in the well being of the family by all of its members.

An additional benefit of a mission statement is that it can help insulate the family from the destructive aspects of mass culture. Many parents ask, "How can we maintain family values which are in opposition to the prevailing culture?" When our children ask us why they can't watch an "R" or "PG 13" rated movie or play a violent video game, or shop for the latest designer label jeans when all their friends are doing it, parents are torn between their personal morality and a fear that their children will be socially isolated if they can't keep up with their peers. The family mission statement provides the necessary support. If each family has its own mission statement, and they do whether or not they actually go through the process of articulating one, then each family is truly unique. Therefore, the reason a parent can offer is that we don't watch R rated movies because they are contrary to what we believe in as a family. It is not an arbitrary prohibition. The only wrinkle here, and it is a healthy wrinkle, is that it pushes us to make sure that our family rules truly make sense. We can't rely on the bumper sticker simplicity, "I'm the mom/dad, that's why." That is a coercive and dogmatic approach that gives parents power only by removing it from their children. When we do this, our children will make other choices, usually inappropriate, to meet their needs for power. In order for rules to work without constant fear-oriented consequences as the sole motivator for compliance, they must be developed in a need fulfilling way and be consistent with the family mission statement.

Don't Stunt Your Growth—
Developing Rules Everyone Can Live By

Social scientists have long recognized how difficult it is to use laws to shape societal norms or to prevent antisocial behavior. Rules imposed by governments and others in power that do not reflect the values of those who the rules are intended to control require the most effort to achieve compliance. Certainly the failure of prohibition is a clear example. The majority of the public did not truly believe that alcohol consumption should be illegal. Therefore, despite extensive law enforcement efforts, drinking thrived while those entrusted with policing the laws were often corrupted in the process. Enforcement of speeding is another example of a rule that apparently does not reflect our values. Many people who are law abiding in every other aspect of their lives knowingly defy speed limits despite the extensive law enforcement and insurance company efforts to curb the behavior. The explanation for this behavior is that the speed limit does not resonate with the beliefs and values of most individuals and, therefore, requires constant coercive tactics to achieve some degree of compliance.

On the other hand, laws that prohibit smoking in confined public places or public nudity require little enforcement because generally speaking most people agree with them. School administrators have long realized that rules to regulate student behavior which are not reflective of the values of the student will call for the most enforcement to achieve compliance. Furthermore, even the effort to force compliance will usually lead to more rule breaking of a different type. That is why it is important in the life of the family to engage all participants in the rule making process.

Creating rules becomes the next topic in the proactive phase of family meetings. The goal is to create rules that are congruent (consistent) with the family mission statement (values) and serve to maximize acceptable need fulfilling behavior without having to resort to authoritarian and coercive punishments. After the mission statement is complete and accepted through consensus decision making, the work on rules begin. Initially, children might not be as concerned about rules as parents. On the surface, children experience rules as a curtailment of their freedom. However, once rules are established according to the Family Centered Parenting model they create the structure necessary for a child to help define his/her life. The framework provides a sense of security which ultimately offers a child more control over his/her environment than a laissez-faire or inconsistent enforcement approach. If we go back to our basic needs model we are reminded that one aspect of power is a sense of control one has over one's environment. If we do not clearly understand the boundaries of our environment then we can never hope to have any sense of control over it. Therefore, rules that are clear and consistently applied define boundaries for children and adults increasing power for both parent and child.

Freedom also increases because the child has defined territory from which to make choices. For example, let us look at 15-year-old Lori coming home from a friend's house on a Friday night. If the family does not have a consistently enforced rule about curfews on Friday nights then Lori will not be sure how late to stay out or what kind of reception she will get when she gets home. One night she might come home at 11:00 and no one objects while on another occasion she is yelled at for coming home at 11:15 because her mother said that 11:15 was too late and that she didn't use good judgment. Lori will not feel free to make choices when the parameters for those choices do not exist. If Lori had been part of proactively establishing an 11:00 curfew the situation would be radically different. First, the curfew rule would be established with input from Lori and a statement from her parents as to why they believe a curfew is necessary. Granting Lori the opportunity to present her view of curfews is empowering to Lori because she will feel worthy of having an opinion that will be listened to by her parents. Her parents will also be empowered because they will have thoughtfully articulated their reasons for how they can best fulfill their roles as parents. When parents feel that they are doing their jobs, their need for power is met. Second, once Lori knows the curfew and feels ownership in establishing it, she has the freedom to choose when she will come home knowing the consequences for her decision making. Experience has shown that if we take the time to establish rules according to Family Centered Parenting, enforcement becomes a relatively minor issue because children no longer seek to increase their power and freedom by challenging rules that they perceive as being arbitrarily conceived and inconsistent with their beliefs and values.

One might justifiably ask, "This sounds fine, but what if parental needs for a rule are in sharp contrast to those expressed by the child?" In the example of Lori and her curfew, let's consider the following scenario:

Lori, her parents Janet and Rob, and her 12-year-old- brother Howie are sitting down for the weekly family meeting. They have a family mission statement in place and agreed at the last meeting that the main topic of this meeting would be family rules. Janet begins by saying that she believes Lori should have a curfew. Lori agrees and says that she thinks 12:30 is appropriate on non-school nights. She says this is the curfew most of her friends have and she thinks it would work out just fine. Bob, a little startled, says that 12:30 is way too late and he thinks 11:00 sounds right. Lori protests and states that her friends would laugh at her if she had to come home at 11:00. Janet offers a compromise of 11:30 and Bob says that is as far as he will go. Bob then asks Lori what she thinks an appropriate consequence should be if she misses her curfew. Lori says, "Do whatever you want, you are obviously in control." Lori pouts and says little for the rest of the meeting. Bob and Janet were feeling ambivalent. On one hand they felt good about having the family hold a meeting and felt that a curfew was established. However, Lori's reaction was troubling. It seemed clear that Lori viewed them as taking control and freedom from her.

There are several ways to look at this situation. The good points are that the family did have the meeting and conducted themselves in a respectful manner consistent with the family mission statement. Janet and Bob did hear what Lori had to say and then stated their limits. Lori was upset but didn't storm out or act inappropriately to her parents or brother. Unfortunately, the potential for a truly need fulfilling meeting for the Lori and her parents was not met. Bob and Janet knew they had gotten their way but it didn't feel right. They simply used their power as adults to impose their views upon Lori. The mission of the family was not to have mom and dad control, but to create an atmosphere where attempts would be made to meet everyone's needs. Lori's behavior indicated that she was not feeling empowered by her parent's decision. In fact one might predict that curfew were going to be a major issue for Lori as she makes behavioral choices that will meet her needs for freedom and power.

Bob and Janet would have benefited from the exercise that follows because it is essential to prepare oneself for a meeting where rules are going to be an issue.

ACTIVITY # 3-2— *Think of a typical rule that might be needed in your family. Examples could be computer usage, curfews, cleaning the bedroom, homework time, etc.*

A working copy of all activities can be found at
www.GrowingGreatRelationships.com

Answer the following questions about the rule:

1. *Do I have standing for this rule?*—This means that logically, not just because you are the parent, that the behavior under consideration is really your business.

2. *What are my needs regarding this rule?*—Be cautious that you are not seeking control simply to feel powerful at the expense of your child and be prepared to honestly defend the legitimacy of your need.

3. *What are my responsibilities regarding this rule?*—The reference is to legal and moral responsibilities relative to the parental role.

4. *How will I determine that the rule agreed upon is a win-win situation?*—What behaviors would I expect from my child if the solution is need fulfilling for him/her and how do I feel about my needs being met.

To help clarify, let us look at some possibilities for each question. In question one the issue of standing is another way of asking who is really affected by the behavior that you are attempting to regulate. A good example is having a child clean his/her bedroom. Before discussing a rule on the subject it is necessary to consider whether or not a rule is really necessary. What impact does it have on a parent if a child does not clean his room? If the answer is that, except for health concerns, only the child will be affected and, therefore, natural consequences will prevail, then a rule might not be needed. After all we learn best when consequences flow entirely from our own behavior and when we are responsible for dealing with those consequences. In the room example we must certainly consider whether or not the child has the capability or resources to accomplish the task and offer help when appropriate. Ultimately, however, the child will inhabit his/her room and although his/her standards might be different than yours, it is not your problem and certainly does not require the time and energy of rule formation and enforcement.

The second question regards parental needs. Before embarking on the rule setting process we need to make sure that our need to have a particular behavior regulated is not based simply on the fact that as a parent we have the power to control the situation. In addition, we need to be clear on what we need to make our lives more enjoyable and fulfilling and that we have a right to express this to our children. The previously mentioned curfew issue is useful for illustration. If Bob told Lori that he needs to go to bed by 11:30 and that before he can fall asleep it is important for him to know that she is home and safe, he is declaring a legitimate parental need. Of course, the statement must be honest and defended. Bob should then follow up with a question to Lori regarding her needs. This leads to a dialogue that hopefully will result in a decision that both parties can live with—which is the essence of a desirable win-win outcome.

Question three deals with formal parental responsibility. It reaches beyond the issue of standing and speaks to legal and moral necessities. At times, we must remind our children that insistence on compliance with a rule is not an issue of preference but of law. A parent has legal responsibilities for a minor child until s/he reaches 18 years of age. It is important to make a child aware that as a parent you are not willing to face the consequences of breaking the law. For example, a teenager refusing to go to school is subjecting the parent to a possible fine for not following the compulsory attendance statutes. If your child says that it is his/her life that is affected by not going to school, s/he needs to be reminded that consequences will fall on the parent and, therefore, must be enforced.

Question four is a monitoring device. It is a method to check that a consensus has been forged. Grudging agreement is often a sign that the individuals are more concerned with moving on than working towards a win-win solution. Win-win doesn't mean that both parties are overjoyed with the result but that the outcome is something that you can both live with and that the solution is need fulfilling. We can determine this by our genuine interest in our children's point of view and honest self-appraisal. For example, a sulking child should be asked if their facial expression reflects dissatisfaction. If the answer is in the affirmative then the family should return to the drawing board to work on the issue. If a child refuses to go further, the parents should simply state that the rule will stand until such a time the child is ready to re-visit the process. Adults also need to expend the energy necessary to make sure that a family rule is also need fulfilling for them. This is often the case when parents reluctantly grant independence to a child before the parent is satisfied that the child can handle his/her new found freedom. In these situations it is legitimate for the parent to express their fears about their child being safe and asking the child what can be done to address the fear. Children in these situations will often help by offering suggestions that grant new freedoms in stages. This gives the parent time to be re-assured that the child is truly responsible.

It is essential to view rule making as a continuous work in progress. Rules should be subject to re-consideration and, if supported by data, be modifiable. This does not mean a rule can be changed unilaterally by either parent or child. However, it does mean that at a family meeting a member of the family is free to discuss possible changes in any previously agreed upon rule by following the same process as was done in creating that rule in the first place. It is also important for rules to be reduced to writing. Young children, and children with disabilities that affect internal self-regulation (e.g., ADHD) need to be able to actually see the rule. Therefore, to help them, rules should be displayed in a prominent place in the home.

There is a tendency in rules systems to pre-negotiate consequences as part of the rule setting process. On the surface this appears to be a logical approach. However, it sends a message that there is an expectation that the rule will be broken. If you didn't think it would be broken you wouldn't need to specify consequences before the fact. Pre-stated consequences are more punishment oriented than discipline oriented because the child breaking the rule receives the specified consequence without taking responsibility for his/her behavior. A preferred method, which will be discussed extensively in a subsequent chapter, assumes that when a rule is broken there is no excuse. The child made a choice to break the rule and needs to commit to a plan for change so that the rule will not be broken again. In addition, the child is required to make restitution for any tangible or intangible loss that occurred as a result of the rule breaking. During the rule making family meeting it is important to discuss the process that will occur if a rule is broken rather than a specific punishment for each rule.

Meetings should end with a formal closure. If the meeting has a set ending time then whoever takes on the role as family timekeeper should give a sign to the facilitator that time is running out. At this point the facilitator should announce that the meeting is coming to a halt and entertain brief feedback from the family as to what was accomplished. If the meeting is not time bound, more responsibility falls on the facilitator to determine that the family is talked out and getting fatigued. Again, the facilitator should seek feedback about the meeting. The last part of the closure routine should be set the time for the next meeting.

A tool for the family to monitor itself is a meeting checklist. As the meeting draws to a conclusion, a designated member of the family should review the following items to make sure the meeting was on target:

A working copy of all activities can be found at
www.GrowingGreatRelationships.com

FAMILY MEETING CHECKLIST *(respond with a Yes or No)*

1. Was the meeting held as scheduled? _____

2. Did all family members attend? _____

3. Were ground rules reviewed? _____

4. Was an agenda prepared? _____

5. Did each family member have the opportunity to contribute to the agenda? _____

6. Did each family member have the opportunity to update the family about happenings in his/her life? _____

7. Did any discussion relate to the family mission statement? _____ (give examples)

8. Does any family member feel that s/he didn't have sufficient opportunity to participate? _____

9. Before bringing the meeting to an end, did the leader check that everyone was "OK" with ending the meeting? _____

10. Did planning take place for the next meeting (scheduling, possible agenda)? _____

It is essential for the family to keep the meeting a sustaining, need fulfilling, and self-correcting process. The meeting is at the heart of Family Centered Parenting and cannot be compromised. Certainly, over time, families begin to develop their own patterns for conducting a meeting. Experienced families often develop a kind of shorthand for communicating with each other. Although this makes meeting times more efficient, it is imperative that as family members become more comfortable with the meeting format the significance of the meeting as a safe, valued family ritual is not diminished. Remember that the time spent as a family in the meeting is precious and highly need fulfilling (love and belonging).

The importance of institutionalizing the family meeting cannot be overemphasized. Clearly, meeting practices and procedures will evolve over time as the family matures. For example, younger family members (five to seven years old) will not have the cognitive abilities to contribute to certain types of discussions like simulations. However their contributions must be acknowledged so that, over time, as they grow they will emerge as eager participants in the full meeting process.

It should be noted that a key ingredient in making meetings truly need fulfilling and efficient is to practice effective communication skills. (Review Chapter 2) The success of family meetings is directly linked to how successful participants can use verbal and non-verbal communication skills to express their needs, desires and thoughts and empathetically respond to each other.

Chapter 4

BRANCHING OUT: FCP IN ACTION

The focus of this chapter is application. That is to learn how to apply the skills previously discussed in order to accomplish broad goals for the family and to learn how to create a road map to navigate through the many issues that must be faced in the life of a family. The key word for meeting both of these objectives effectively and efficiently is process.

It should be noted that there is a fundamental distinction between the words "effective" and "efficient" and that that difference is extremely important in parenting. Effectiveness relates to how well you meet your goal while efficient relates to the speed and resources expended to meet that goal. In parenting terms, it might be efficient to gain compliance to a parental request from a six-year-old with a threat or a quick slap to the rear end. However, if our goal is to teach our child responsible decision making, this strategy will not further that end. Conversely, devoting four or five hours of family meetings to get a child to take out the garbage without reminders would be an example of an effective approach in that the goal of completing this chore without coercion has been accomplished. However, this appears to be highly inefficient because of the vast amount of time invested for such a limited result. In essence, we are now at the point in Family Centered Parenting where we can work on combining effectiveness with the techniques needed to be highly efficient.

Frankly, the major reason families are unable to sustain a new approach to their parenting is because they have not mastered the skills needed to efficiently implement the necessary changes. The inefficiency leads them to the conclusion that the new approach is simply not worth the time and effort. They then quickly retreat to the patterns of the past. It should be noted that when we begin to implement Family Centered Parenting strategies it might feel inefficient because of the time needed to put the process in place. Spending five or six hours of meetings to arrive at a three-sentence mission statement certainly smacks of inefficiency. However, be mindful that an initial investment of time, "front loading" will ultimately lead to efficiency down the road. Consider the steps taken at the beginning as a training period. Enterprises that invest heavily in research and development and training are usually the leaders in their fields. As a family, the commitment to planning, and training is a necessary requirement which will, in a relatively short time, begin to yield an increase in both quality time and empowerment for parents and children.

As indicated, there is no one technique or practice that can be neatly applied to each given family situation or issue. Human beings and family systems are frankly far too complicated to expect a "one size fits all" approach to problem resolution. The image comes to mind of a stressed mom wandering down the aisles of the supermarket with two kids in tow responding to her six-year-old stridently demanding a box of cookies. She then tells her kids to hold on as she struggles to reach into her bag for her parenting manual to look up the right response for the situation. This is obviously an absurd picture for two reasons. First, there is the assumption that there is a "right" answer. Unfortunately, too many parenting "experts"—a term that includes everyone from child psychologists to Aunt Betty—would lead you to think that each specific situation has a desired programmed response. We are far too variable in our individual needs and far too governed by specific situations for this to be true. Second, even if there were a so called "best" response for a given situation, under the pressures of day-to-day living, it is hardly reasonable to expect a parent to either remember or research the so called best answer. Instead, what we must rely on and commit to is a process of need fulfilling goal attainment and problem solving that will encompass the variety of situations and individual differences among children and adults, yet still provide a focused direction or system for dealing with our issues.

The first part of the process is being proactive. Proactive is the buzzword for prevention and basically refers to planning ahead or anticipating situations. The better we are as family members in preparing for what lies ahead the better we are able to avoid conflict and crisis.

Let us return to the harried mom in the supermarket for illustration:

Prevention of the supermarket incident begins with anticipation. Based on past experience, Mom knows that little Sally will make many demands for things when they go shopping. Therefore, Mom should start her processing with Sally in the car before they get to the market. The dialogue might go something like this. "Sally, where are we going?" Sally answers, "Food shopping." Mom says, "What are our rules for the supermarket and what will we do if the rules are not followed?"

(Note: Mom is not asking Sally for a specific consequence for breaking the rule. She is preparing Sally for the process that they will go through if the rule is broken.)

There is an additional level of prevention underlying this scenario because we are assuming that mom and Sally have discussed supermarket rules at a family meeting and that the dialogue in the car is intended to review or rehearse not to acquire new information. This underscores the importance of being proactive. By making the investment in time and energy of holding family meetings where rules and expectations can be discussed in a non-crisis atmosphere we set the stage for reminders and ultimately for accountability. When children have input in formulating a rule and then are given the opportunity to review the rule before the upcoming event we leave no excuses for not complying with that rule.

Before we get too crazy about making rules for every eventuality, which is impossible, remember that rules must be responsive to the unique needs of each family. As noted, children have different temperaments and vary in their need for external reminders. For example, a child diagnosed with ADHD needs constant reminders including visual cues as to rules for varying situations. The disorder interferes with a child's ability to self-regulate, thereby requiring heavy emphasis on rules before engaging in a specific activity.

As children grow older, we can rely on more general or moral codes of behavior that are less dependent on rules for specific situations like behaving in the supermarket. Family meetings are a place where families can discuss morality as it relates to the mission statement of the family. As children age their ability to understand ethical behavior increases from a fear of getting caught level to a fairly sophisticated personal morality. With this in mind, a more global set of standards, (the golden rule, Ten Commandments), can become an on-going focus for discussion at meetings. This helps children to behave responsibly in a variety of circumstances by giving them a frame of reference to determine if their behavior, or intended behavior when there is no specific rule to rely on, is consistent with their values.

Let us imagine your nine-year-old son playing with his friends in your neighbor's back yard. A boy from down the street takes your son's baseball glove without his permission and runs home. Your son finds out who took the glove and heads after the thief. He gets to the thief's house and rings the bell. The young man comes to the door and asks him what he wants. Your son asks for his glove back and the other boy says he doesn't know anything about the glove. Your son is ready to enter the house and punch the boy.

It would be hard to anticipate this situation and therefore it is extremely unlikely that a rule has been established for your son to follow under these circumstances. However, he still has to make a choice about his behavior and needs guidelines for making that choice. As a family, if the broader principle of when to use physical force to solve problems has been addressed as part of establishing family values, your son can then draw upon these principles to direct his behavior. In this situation, if your son believes in a family value which dictates that one only uses violence in those rare cases of pure self-defense, he can then rely on this concept when he decides not to hit the other child and instead to choose alternatives that are consistent with his values.

It would certainly be appropriate at this point to start talking about the issue of problem resolution and what to do when things aren't going smoothly. Despite our best efforts as parents, at times, our children will make mistakes. We hope that the natural consequences of their errors are not too severe and that a mistake creates an opportunity for learning. Someone once said that a mistake is only a failure if we don't learn from it. Therefore, as parents we need to create routines for problem solving that opens the door for mistakes to become learning experiences. It should be emphasized that parents also have to own up to their mistakes and model for their children how they have learned from them. This teaches children that people aren't perfect and that despite one's best efforts, we do make mistakes. Furthermore, we also can discuss with our children and at times even seek their advice on how an adult mistake can be corrected in the most responsible manner.

Stormy Days—Problem Solving Meetings

The problem solving family meeting is one alternative method for responding to mistakes. If a situation becomes known to the parents that their child has made a mistake by breaking a rule or behaving in a way which is contrary to their family's values, and that an immediate response is not needed, then the family meeting format can be utilized for problem solving. The family meeting has some distinct advantages for problem solving. First, it provides some separation between the triggering incident and its resolution. This time creates opportunities for reflection and consideration of alternative approaches for resolving the issue at hand. Second, it makes the entire family part of the problem solving experience. This fosters highly need fulfilling (love & belonging) connections among family members. In other words, it creates ownership in the problem and its solution and makes the family a team that meets the challenges of life as a family unit of interdependent parts. In a sense this supports a family culture where expectations are shared and all family members have a responsibility for ensuring responsible behavior. The role of the family is now extended from rule formation to rule monitoring and when needed, correction.

The problem solving family meeting does present some unique challenges. To begin with, it is crucial that problem solving meetings aren't the most predominant type of meeting held. If this is the case, we create an anticipatory stressful association with meetings. Meetings in general must be broadly need fulfilling and provide for fun needs as well as the other three basic needs. As the family matures in practicing Family Centered Parenting, all members must be vigilant that they don't lose sight of the overall purpose of meetings by holding meetings only when a problem or crisis occurs. In addition, the problem solving simulations that are done in routine family meetings can now be applied to real life situations. By rehearsing possible scenarios, the family builds a reference base for dealing with actual issues.

An illustration should be helpful:

Sandra, a 12 year old, is in the midst of a personal dilemma. There is a girl, Rachel, in her math class who Sandra likes and wants to get to know better. Rachel is part of the most popular group in middle school. During lunch, Rachel asked Sandra if she could see her math homework. Sandra said sure and then watched as Rachel copied all of her answers. Sandra said nothing. Two days later Rachel again asked Sandra to see her homework. Sandra complied and again watched Rachel copy her answers. The next day, after inviting Sandra to a party at her house on Friday night, Rachel again asked to see the math homework. Sandra reluctantly gave her the homework. That night, Sandra mentioned the problem to her mother. Her mother recalled that several months ago at a family meeting they had simulated (role-played) a very similar situation. Sandra remembered the role-play and told her mother she knew what she had to do. She got on the telephone and called Rachel and using a version of the dialogue rehearsed at the family meeting was able to tell Rachel in a non-confrontational way why she was uncomfortable about sharing homework on a regular basis. Rachel seemed to hear Sandra without getting angry.

When Sandra was reminded of the role-play, she was empowered to deal with her situation. Her ability to handle the matter independently will go a long way to build her self-esteem. Here, the family meeting discussion of a hypothetical situation served as a springboard for solving a real problem.

Common sense tells us that the problem solving family meeting is likely to be emotionally charged. As we have learned, individuals who are in an emotionally volatile state tend not to think too clearly. This is especially true if some or all of the participants are directly involved in the problem as is often the case when a parent brings an issue concerning a rule violation to the table or when there is a dispute among siblings. Therefore, it is essential that the participants prepare for this likelihood. Preparation starts at the beginning of the meeting with a review of the ground rules for exchanging ideas. This is crucial, especially when it is known in advance that there is a disagreement. The rules that should be stressed are those that relate to appropriate ways of expressing anger, responding to hurtful comments, the use of profanity, and raising one's voice. The effective communication practices, particularly seeking to understand before being understood and the validation of feelings, should also be stressed before problem solving begins.

The next part of the agenda is a clear statement of the problem in descriptive not judgmental language. The facilitator, in this case a parent is probably the best choice, should take a fairly active role in monitoring the ground rules and when needed in re-directing participants with reminders. When the individuals who are the focus of the meeting are finished with describing the situation, the facilitator should paraphrase what they heard and ask if s/he got it right.

Let us look at a fairly common family situation as an illustration:

Samantha is a fifteen year old who, as a typical teenager, spends a considerable amount of time on the computer. Her twelve-year-old brother, Danny, is starting to increase his computer use. Danny and Samantha share the household computer that their parents placed in the family room. Lately, Danny has been nagging Samantha to get off the computer. She gets angry and yells back at him to leave her alone and wait for her to finish. The problem has escalated to fairly constant bickering between Samantha and Danny over the use of the computer. Their mother has had it with the constant arguing and has called a family meeting to discuss the situation. She checks everyone's calendar and there is agreement that the meeting will be held at 7:30 that evening. Although it is Samantha's turn to facilitate the meeting, mom realizes that since Samantha is part of the problem, she will lead the meeting.

> **Mom**— *"I asked for the meeting because I am uncomfortable with the constant bickering between Samantha and Danny. I find it very unpleasant to live in a house with this much disharmony. In addition, our family mission statement states that we will treat each other with respect. I don't feel this is happening."*

(Mom has stated the problem utilizing "I" statements and she clearly established her basis for asking for the meeting. Her mention of the family mission statement is important as it ties the current issue with agreed upon family principles)

> **Dad**— *"Before we get going, I think it is important to re-state our discussion ground rules. I believe there is a good chance there are some angry feelings here and they need to be handled according to our rules. Danny, would you be willing to begin?"*

(Dad interjects the importance of ground rules in a problem solving meeting where tempers may flare. He also validates the fact that there are angry feelings involved. Lastly, he invites Danny to speak, he doesn't demand)

DANNY— *"OK, Dad. No name calling or interrupting. Use describing words not judging words. If we are feeling angry, stop and get calm before we continue. Let me tell you that it won't be easy because Samantha is being a real brat about this."*

SAMANTHA— *"Did you hear that? He called me a brat. That is against our rules."*

DAD— *"Thank you, Samantha, for pointing that out. Danny you did re-state our rules accurately. Good job. What about your last comment?"*

DANNY— *"Sorry, that was against the rules. I shouldn't have used the word brat to Samantha."*

(Dad provides praise to Danny that is appropriate. Danny is held accountable by his sister for name-calling. Dad addresses Danny by allowing Danny to take responsibility.)

MOM— *"Samantha, please tell us what is going on with the computer."*

SAMANTHA— *"I have a lot of research for my homework and I also like to catch up with friends. Danny interrupts me and that embarrasses me and makes it hard to concentrate. When he does that I sometimes get even by not getting off the computer. I need my own laptop."*

MOM— *"Samantha, I heard you say that computer time is important to you and that Danny nagging you and asking for the computer causes* *you to feel embarrassed and disrupts your concentration. I would suggest that before you propose a solution, we make sure we all understand the problem. Did I summarize your point of view accurately?"*

(Mom paraphrases and checks for understanding. She also re-directed Samantha about being premature with suggestions for fixing the problem)

SAMANTHA— *"That's about right."*

MOM— *"Danny, what do you have to say?"*

DANNY— *"I don't think it is fair that she spends more time on the computer than I do. When I need the computer she should get off and let me use it."*

DAD— *"Danny, I heard you say that you believe Samantha is using the computer more than you are and that when you ask her to use it, she should just let you have it. Did I get it right?'*

DANNY— *"Yeah."*

MOM— *"Samantha, do you want to add anything before we start finding solutions."*

SAMANTHA— *"No."*

(Mom has completed the clarification of the problem stage. She is ready to move the family to seeking solutions)

We are now at the next phase of the problem solving family meeting—seeking alternative solutions. Since the problem has been clarified, and all parties were heard and understood the family is ready to seek alternative solutions through brainstorming. As you may remember, brainstorming is a process to freely generate alternatives. Initially, in order to encourage participation and creativity, ideas are not evaluated. After the list of alternatives is completed, discussion is held on each item until a consensus is reached as to the best course of action. Results should be recorded for the sake of accountability. It is also helpful to build in a feedback mechanism so that progress can be monitored with adjustments made when needed.

> **MOM**— *"We are ready to start looking for solutions. Remember we are brainstorming so that there is no comment, except to seek clarification, for any stated suggestion. I'll keep track of our alternatives on this chart."*

(Mom re-stated the rules for brainstorming. She also continued as facilitator by volunteering to chart the answers.)

> **SAMANTHA**— *"Have Danny ask me politely if he could please have the computer as soon as I am finished."*

> **DANNY**— *"Get one of us a laptop then Samantha and I will each have access to a computer at the same time."*

> **DAD**— *"Create a schedule for who has primary use of the computer at a particular hour."*

> **MOM**— *"I like Dad's suggestion. Are there any other suggestions? Let me review the list with you and then we can start the evaluation process."*

> **DAD**— *"Another computer would be ideal, but the family budget is not able to cover the costs right now."*

(Dad provides feedback as to limits in the decision making.)

DANNY— *"If she (Samantha) promises to get off the computer within 15 minutes, I can promise to ask politely."*

SAMANTHA— *"Dad, how about if I contribute part of my allowance and what I will be earning this summer babysitting towards a laptop. Can I then get one as a Christmas present? If that's OK, I can probably do more texting and give Danny more access for the time being."*

DAD— *"Samantha that's a workable plan. If Mom agrees I can go along with you paying half of the cost of a new laptop."*

MOM— *"I think that Samantha is on target. We can work out the costs. In the meantime, can we agree that Danny will ask politely while Samantha agrees to get off the computer within 15 minutes and she will use more texting. I will write this down for the record. Also, we will discuss this issue within a week to see how it is going and whether we need modifications."*

ALL— *"OK"*

(Mom brings the meeting to closure with a summary of the agreement. She seeks a consensus and records the results. In addition, she arranges for another meeting to monitor results.)

When Lightening Strikes: Problem Solving On The Go

We are now ready to tackle problem solving in situations where either timing or the scope of the problem does not lend itself to the meeting format. As parents, there are numerous circumstances that require our immediate intervention and can't be deferred for resolution at a formal family meeting. These are generally issues that require a solution at the moment or involve a fairly straightforward rule violation, which is more of an issue of individual responsibility than an issue for the whole family to deal with. It should be noted that this does not preclude asking for a meeting after the event as part of the overall problem solving process.

The goal of the intervention is discipline—defined as teaching responsible behavior. Remember, we are not just seeking the end of the inappropriate behavior in question but are creating the space for the child to take responsibility for that behavior, and even more importantly, for not repeating that behavior. Although it might appear inefficient on the surface because of the extra processing time, in the long run there will be fewer recurrences requiring parental intervention. Therefore, as is the case with problem solving family meetings, an initial investment of time in processing will lead to less overall time being devoted to responding to inappropriate behaviors. It will also become obvious as the four steps are explained that they cannot be put into practice without the foundation that has been set down in the family meeting process.

THE FOLLOWING FOUR-STEP model is suggested when action must be taken.

1. Ask the child, **"What are you doing?"** or **"What Happened?"**— Even though it might seem obvious, it is essential for the child to identify his/her own behavior. The child's description will set the stage for comparison in the next step.

2. Ask the child, **"Is (was) your behavior consistent with our rules or values? How is not?"**—We are now asking the child to make a

value judgment about his/her behavior. In addition, if there was a miscommunication regarding expectations, this is the place for the child to make his/her case. If the parent feels the child's argument is valid; the matter can then be referred to a family meeting for discussion. However, generally speaking, one should not expect excuses. There is a known rule or expectation and the chosen behavior violated that rule or expectation. That is the essence of the value judgment.

3. Ask the child, "What need were you trying to meet with your chosen behavior and what were the **consequences for this choice?**"—This question goes to the heart of the Family Centered Parenting process. We are asking the child to demonstrate his/her understanding that all behaviors are based on choices and are need fulfilling. Therefore, the behavior being discussed had a purpose but the choice made to fulfill that purpose was against established rules/expectations and had negative consequences. Obviously, to answer the question, the child has to have an understanding of basic needs theory. The assumption is that this has been done at regular family meetings prior to the incident.

4. Ask the child, "What can you do in the future to meet your need(s) in a way that is consistent with our rules or values?"—This is the commitment phase of the process. Here we are recognizing that the underlying needs that caused the behavioral choice do not go away and that different behavioral choices must be made which are need fulfilling and align more closely with understood rules, values and expectations. The degree of detail required of the child will naturally

depend on the nature of the behavior and whether or not it has previously occurred.

An illustration should prove helpful:

Claudia, her husband, Derek, and their two children, Keisha, age 11, and Derek Jr., age 8, are visiting Claudia's sister, Loraine, for Sunday dinner. Loraine and her husband have three children who are all older than Derek Jr. At the dinner table, there is much conversation about what the various children are doing. Loraine's kids are athletes and honor role students and she does have a habit of overdoing her description of their accomplishments. After about an hour of eating and conversation Derek Jr., for no apparent reason, deliberately knocks over his sister's drink into her lap. Keisha jumps out of her seat and yells at Derek Jr. for what he did. Conversation stops and everyone turns to Derek Jr. Claudia turns to Derek Jr. and asks:

SCENARIO A

CLAUDIA— *"Why did you knock over your sister's drink?"*

DEREK, JR.— *"She gave me a look"*

DEREK— *"That's no excuse. Leave the table and sit in the living room by yourself. You will miss dessert."*

DEREK JR. — *"That's not fair."*

CLAUDIA— *"Listen to your father right now or you will lose television privileges tonight."*

Derek Jr. leaves the room.

This is a fairly typical parental response. A child misbehaves and the parents respond with a punishment. There is some complaint from the child but the fear of further punishment insures compliance. On the positive side, a child's misbehavior was not ignored. Parents responded swiftly and dealt with the situation in an efficient manner. Violence was not needed and the child did ultimately comply with the punishment by leaving the table. The problem with this approach is that although expedient one can ask, "What was the origin of the behavior? What has the child learned from this experience?" and "What is the probability of a similar situation happening again?"

SCENARIO B— *Claudia turns to Derek Jr. and asks him to come with her to the kitchen for a moment.*

CLAUDIA— *"What Happened?"*

DEREK JR.— *"I knocked over Keisha's soda after she gave me a dirty look."*

CLAUDIA— *"Was deliberately knocking over her drink appropriate and following our family rules about responding to something your sister might have done?"*

DEREK JR.— *"I guess not."*

CLAUDIA— *"What need were you trying to meet with your behavior and what were the consequences for this choice?"*

DEREK JR.— *"I guess I was annoyed because no one was paying any attention to me. When I knocked over Keisha's glass everyone turned to me."*

CLAUDIA— *"And that had to do with which need?"*

DEREK JR.— *"When I am ignored I don't feel important. It must be my power need."*

CLAUDIA— *"I agree. What consequence did you get for choosing to get power this way?"*

DEREK JR.— *"I feel embarrassed and my sister is mad at me. After we are done talking I have to go back and face everyone."*

CLAUDIA— *"What other choices could you make and that will get you attention and will not have negative consequences?*

DEREK JR.—*"I could have said excuse me and asked someone if they wanted to hear about what I am doing in school."*

CLAUDIA— *"I agree. If you would like help with doing that I can help you stop the conversation. Let's go back and you can try it out. You did a great job in working through what happened. What can you do about your sister?"*

DEREK JR.— *"I'll tell Keisha that I am sorry."*

Let us examine the major differences between scenarios A & B. Clearly B will probably take up more time than A. Although more efficient in the short run, A is a punishment oriented intervention which does little to promote growth and long term changes in behavior. In B, a practical application of the four-step intervention model, we see the parent engage in discipline as a leader and teacher rather than as a punisher. The first thing Claudia does is to ask her son to leave the table. This gives them a chance to process the incident without an audience. The question, "What happened?"

does not presume anything and, therefore, reduces the need for a defensive response. It places the burden on the child to use his own words to describe his behavior. In the next question, Claudia seeks a value judgment from her son. She is asking him to compare his described behavior with the values, rules and expectations of the family. This step serves first to clear up any ambiguities. Occasionally, a child will reasonably not be aware that the behavior he describes is contrary to expectations or established rules. If this is the case, the parent can halt the process, indicate that this matter will be discussed at a future family meeting and until such time as it is clarified, the expectation for appropriate behavior is as follows. In most cases there are no loopholes for the child to use as an excuse and s/he makes the value judgment on him/herself. It is essential for building a sense of personal responsibility that the child judge himself rather than be judged by a parent. Claudia also did something that was noteworthy and showed that she utilized effective communication practices. She acknowledged that Keisha might have done something to provoke the situation. By saying, "…. responding to something your sister might have done?" Claudia is validating the fact that Keisha might have done something but is not offering this as an excuse for Derek's inappropriate behavior. The validation facilitates Derek's non-defensive response.

Claudia now shifts to seeking the underlying root of Derek's behavior. Her next question, utilizing the key words of "needs" and "choice" stresses the hard work of discipline. Derek has to think about his behavior in terms of being a choice over which he has control. Furthermore, that choice is linked to his ability to get his needs met. As indicated, previous learning about needs must have taken place prior to this being a reasonable question. Again, the family meeting serves as a place for us to teach our children about basic needs theory. The more effectively we do this, the more efficient we will be when we are involved in a discipline dialogue. Derek does a good job of linking attention seeking to an attempt to gain power. Claudia then counters with a follow-up question about the consequences he experienced for this choice. Derek accurately describes the result of his behavior. A strong link of accountability has now been established. Claudia now begins to focus on the future. Her question is seeking an informal plan from Derek that acknowledges that the need will not go away but that there are acceptable/appropriate behaviors, which he can choose, that will meet his needs. Claudia verifies Derek's plan and offers assistance as a resource to help him accomplish it. She then follows with a statement of praise that is proportional to the situation. Lastly, Claudia reminds Derek that he has taken something away from his sister. By calling her a name she has been diminished and Derek offers to apologize. This is called restitution and is an important element in Family Centered Parenting and will be discussed further when we examine the more formal written plan model.

Overall, Claudia's response to her son's misbehavior in situation "B" should go a long way in insuring responsible behavior in her son. Derek's involvement was substantial and clearly a learning experience. However, there are no guarantees that this will not happen again. Derek's power needs must be met and, as a family, this must be addressed in order to avoid recurrences in inappropriate behaviors.

The scenario in B does have limitations beyond the fact that it is somewhat more time consuming than punishment. It is useful for a quick response for a relatively minor misbehavior, but is too superficial for more serious matters. What follows is an expanded formal version of the four-step approach called "The Plan." It is an elaboration of the informal model which squarely addresses the issue of restitution and seeks a commitment for change in written form in order to create a record that reinforces the concept of accountability.

A working copy of all activities can be found at
www.GrowingGreatRelationships.com

THE PLAN—
Applying Discipline When Most Needed

1. What did I do? _____

_____

_____

2. Was that act or behavior consistent with our rules and expectations? How was it not? _____

_____

_____

3. What need(s) was I trying to satisfy with this behavior? Explain. ___

_____

_____

4. What are the negative consequences of meeting my needs this way?

_____

_____

5. How can I make things right to those who have lost something because of my behavior? _____

_____

_____

6. What is my plan to meet my needs in a way which fits better with our rules and values? _____

_____

_____

Date _____ Child _____ Parent _____

PAGE 2 OF The Plan

Basic Needs

POWER— *control, importance, respect, value, self-worth, attention*

FREEDOM— *able to choose, make decisions, expressing yourself*

LOVE & BELONGING— *cared about, friendship, caring about others*

FUN— *pleasure, playful, creative, energetic, joyful*

SURVIVAL— *safe*

Making Things Right (restitution)

Make up time or labor.

Payment for damaged or destroyed items.

Demonstrating caring, to the victim's satisfaction, about the hurt feelings and/or loss of face to the victim which was caused by your behavior.

Service to the school or community.

Making yourself a more worthwhile person.

The Plan—Applying Discipline When Most Needed is based on six questions and requires that the answers be written down. The age of the child and his/her ability to utilize written language will dictate the degree of independence expected from a child as s/he completes the worksheet. Regardless of whether the responses are dictated by the child and written by the parent or written by the child, the intervention should conclude with a written document that should be retained by the parents.

The Plan should be used when, in the judgment of the parent, the misbehavior is of severe enough nature to require a formal record or it is responding to a behavior that although relatively minor has occurred before. As we go through the document, these distinctions should become clearer. The first four questions on The Plan are essentially the same as the four steps in the informal approach. The difference, as is readily apparent, is that the worksheet permits the child to, if he or she is capable, complete the exercise independently before parent review. The advantage is that a child working by himself will tend to feel independent and responsible. The parent is not controlling the situation but acting as a leader and resource if the child gets stuck. Completing The Plan worksheet with little adult supervision becomes highly need fulfilling for the child. Both power needs and freedom needs are met when a child is able to do his/her plan without outside pressure.

Number five on the worksheet presents a significant difference from the informal approach. Although touched upon in the four-step model, here the concept of restitution takes on a much larger role. Restitution or restoration is an attempt to make things right to those who have sustained a loss as a result of our behavior. The concept of restoration is at the core of responsibility. When an individual attempts to right a wrong to the maximum extent possible, s/he is owning the behavior, realizing that the behavior had an effect on another individual and that the proper course of action is to find a way to give back what has been lost. The forms of restitution that are easiest to figure out are those that involve a material loss. For example, if a child breaks his brother's toy or because of inappropriate behavior damages a piece of furniture, restitution is usually accomplished by actually replacing the object or contributing money to fixing it. When the loss does not involve a physical object, we need to be a little more creative in our restitution planning.

In the life of a family, hurtful comments, especially between siblings, are often part of a problem situation. Although "I'm sorry" is the obvious restitution this might prove insufficient as restitution. Certainly an apology is the first step, but only the person who has been the recipient of an insult can say whether or not they feel whole again. Therefore, it is suggested that when restitution involves name-calling, the perpetrator must ask the victim if the apology is sufficient. If the victim says no, the next question should be, "What else can I do to help repair any damage I have done." Operationally, The Plan should state, "I will apologize and ask if there is anything else I can do to make up for the hurt I caused." Brainstorming alternative approaches at a non-problem solving family meeting to restoring a person after a hurtful comment will add to the skills of the child when they are actually working on a plan.

What is often lost when a child behaves inappropriately is parental time. For example, if a parent has to go to school to see a teacher because of an incident or a parent has to go to another child's house to pick her child up because of a dispute, it is parental time that is lost. Another example would be the time spent on resolving a dispute between siblings. Sorting out the situation and monitoring plans with the children can be quite time consuming. In these situations it is recommended that when a parent reaches question 5, they look for a restoration of their time. An example might be a child doing a chore for a parent that they wouldn't normally perform. This gives the parent back time to spend as s/he sees fit and compensates for the loss of time created by the child's inappropriate behavior.

The first five questions lead to the question 6, the seeking of a commitment for change. The essence of discipline is to have learned something from the misdeed and we evidence this learning by changing our behavior. Question 6 asks the child to offer a plan for change that is need fulfilling and is consistent with family rules and expectations. This is not an easy task and will often require considerable coaching from a parent. The first part picks up on the answer provided in question 3. The need has been identified and now we are validating the fact that the need doesn't go away. The Plan for change must be linked to this need in order for it to be effective. Furthermore, The Plan must be consistent with established rules and expectations. Merely substituting one inappropriate behavior for another will not do the trick. Again, creativity on the part of the child and parent is important. Previous discussion and practice through simulations at family meetings will help the child in coming up with solutions.

An example of a situation and a plan to address it might help to further clarify the process:

The Mall

Howard is a 14-year-old high school freshman. On Friday, Howard asked his mother, Ellen, if he could go home on the bus with his friend Larry and then go to the high school football game directly from Larry's house. He said that Larry's parents would drive him home after the game that should end by 9:30. Ellen agreed. Howard came home at 10:00 and said the game went into overtime. He said the game was great and that he was very tired. He went to bed. On Saturday morning, Ellen's sister-in-law called and said that she thought she saw Howard hanging out outside the mall last night. He was with a group of about 10 other teenagers and they were passing around several brown paper bags. Many of them were also smoking. When she approached the group and called Howard's name, one boy wearing a green Jets jacket ran from the group and headed into the mall.

She was reasonably sure it was Howard. Howard wore his Jets jacket to school on Friday. Helen hung up the phone and headed for Howard's room.

ELLEN— *I am enraged. I feel betrayed by my son and embarrassed in front of my sister-in-law, Phyllis. Phyllis likes to remind me that she I am too easy on Howard. Howard is generally not a problem. However, since 8th grade he has become more focused on his friends and shares very little with the family. He started high school two months ago and has attempted to extend his curfew and be granted more independence. At the last family meeting I told him that, depending on his grades on the first report card, I might agree to greater freedom. I am heading upstairs to his room to let him have it.*

HOWARD— *Mom just stormed into my room and shut my stereo. She looks really pissed off. She is ranting about a phone call from Aunt Phyllis and the mall. I guess I was spotted. I am not going to kiss anyone's behind. I am old enough to go to the mall instead of a dumb football game. I will be probably accused of drinking which I don't do. She won't believe me. She thinks I am a liar. If she tries to ground me I'll just work around it. The more she tries to treat me like a baby the more I want to show her I am growing up. She has no right to barge into my room and shut my music. She better get out of here.*

ELLEN— *My throat hurts from shouting. I am getting nowhere and I better get out of here and relax. Five minutes pass. I feel calmer. Let me use the techniques of Family Centered Parenting. I'm going back to his room with The Plan. This time I am going to knock and ask if I can come in for a discussion. After all, I would expect him to knock on my bedroom door before I came in.*

HOWARD— *She is knocking on the door now. I guess I better deal with her.*

Before we apply the planning model to this situation we should first look at Ellen's initial approach to the events. Hearing the news from her sister-in-law triggered strong feelings in Ellen. Her quality world picture of herself as a parent was challenged. As a "good" (in control) parent she expected her son to follow through on expectations and not to deceive her. In addition, her sister-in-law's image of her as a lax parent struck home. Ellen's power need increased as her sense of worth as a parent plummeted. Therefore, it is not unexpected that she reacted with anger. Anger is a way of empowering ourselves and is an emotion that often flows from an affront to our self-esteem. Unfortunately, her anger provoked a defensive reaction in Howard and there was a scene. In her state of anger, she was not able to apply her problem solving skills. By withdrawing until she calmed down, she was then able to think more clearly and return to deal with the problem in a thoughtful way.

ELLEN— *"Howard, I got a call from Aunt Phyllis this morning. She said that she is pretty sure that she saw you by the mall last night. She saw someone who looked like you wearing a Jets jacket. When she called your name the person she saw turned around and headed for the mall entrance. What happened last night? Before you answer, I want to let you know that I will follow the questions on The Plan. I'll write down whatever you say."*

(Good use of descriptive language. No accusations thereby opening the way for an honest reply. Ellen decides to let Howard dictate answers since the circumstances are not sufficiently clear).

HOWARD— *"I decided not to go to the football game. Larry's mom took us to the mall instead and then his dad drove me home."*

ELLEN— *"Aunt Phyllis said that she saw some boys passing around a paper bag. She thought they were drinking and also smoking cigarettes."*

(Ellen attempts to get the whole story on the table).

HOWARD— *"I don't drink or smoke but a couple of guys were smoking and passing around a wine cooler."*

ELLEN— *"Thank you for being honest. Since I don't have any other evidence I will accept your word that you weren't drinking or smoking. However, was your behavior consistent with our rules?"*

(Ellen gives positive reinforcement for Howard's straight answer. She also acknowledges that she will not accuse him of wrongdoing without evidence. This helps to empower Howard because he was trusted.)

HOWARD— *"No. I'm supposed to let you know if my plans change. Also I need to get permission from you to go to the mall. But, Mom, I think I am old enough to change plans without asking as long as I come home at the right time."*

ELLEN— *"We can discuss changing rules later. Right now we are dealing with breaking a rule that you knew."*

(Ellen avoids Howard's deflection and re-directs him to making a value judgment)

ELLEN— *"Please explain what need you were attempting to meet with this behavior."*

HOWARD— *"That's a no brainer, my need for freedom."*

ELLEN— *"I agree. What are the consequences for attempting to meet your need this way?"*

HOWARD— *"Having this conversation. Giving Aunt Phyllis another reason to bug you."*

ELLEN— *"That sounds right. What about my ability to trust you?*

HOWARD— *"I really didn't think of that."*

(Ellen has pinpointed a loss. This sets up the next question.)

ELLEN— *"How can you make things right."*

HOWARD— *"I'm sorry I broke my trust mom. I won't do it again."*

ELLEN— *"I appreciate that but I still have a problem with Aunt Phyllis."*

(Ellen validates Howard but pushes the issue based on her own needs)

HOWARD— *"I'll call Aunt Phyllis and tell her why I ran into the mall."*

ELLEN — *"That's great. As far as my trust in you, it will take a little time for you to earn it again. I hope this can happen."*

(Ellen praises Howard and clarifies that restitution to her will be an on-going issue)

ELLEN— *"How are you going to get that freedom need met without violating rules?"*

> **HOWARD**— *"How about sitting down with you and coming up with a contract about my curfew and reporting responsibilities."*
>
> **ELLEN**— *"I can live with that. When are we going to do that?"*
>
> **HOWARD**— *"How about Sunday night before our family meeting?"*
>
> **ELLEN**— *"Sounds good. Please read and sign The Plan if you think it is accurate. Then I'll sign it."*

(Ellen is holding Howard accountable by asking for a specific time for discussing the broader issues of freedom. Asking him to sign The Plan after he reads it provides documentation for the future.)

Ellen made several decisions in this process. First, she chose to have Howard dictate the answers instead of having him do it, or at least begin it, independently. This is a judgment call made on a number of factors including the ability of the child to express him/herself in writing, the child's level of experience with the planning process and the nature of the situation at hand. As a rule of thumb, the less ambiguous the problem the easier it is for the child to attempt The Plan on his/her own. Second, the commitment made in response to question 6 was not in of itself a plan for change. It triggered an additional meeting to explore the matter in more depth. Ellen's decision helped put closure to the problem at hand without compromising the necessity to have a carefully negotiated more permanent conclusion.

The importance of having the child and the parent sign The Plan and then save it cannot be underestimated. The Plan is to be treated as a quasi-legal document within the world of the family and serves to foster accountability. When a parent makes the decision to have a child complete a plan, former plans must be reviewed for similarities. A completed plan becomes a reference point for a future commitment. For example, imagine that a child in a previous plan, which grew out of an incident of profanity directed at her brother, committed to not doing it again by virtue of exercising willpower. Although somewhat skeptical, the parent accepted this commitment even though they had little faith it would work. When the situation occurs again, the child should be directed to back to her original plan with the question, "Did your last plan to use willpower work?" Since it clearly didn't work, the responsibility is now placed back on the child to come up with a plan that is more rigorous than the previous attempt. The filing of previous plans and maintaining their availability for reference reinforces the principle that there are no excuses. The premise is that we keep working until we get it right. In addition, experience will show that the more need fulfilling the commitment, the better the chances are that it will be successful. The Plans that have to be redone are usually focused more on behaving than finding alternate means to meet needs. This again underscores the importance of learning needs theory and rehearsing possible hypothetical situations in the family meeting.

It would be helpful at this point to devote some time to the process of contracting. Contracting is a valuable device that may be used as an extension of a plan for change, as in the previous example, or it might flow from parental or child request as a means to create limits or rules before a situation arises. Essentially, a contract between parent and child is a negotiated agreement of expectations for both parties. It is usually reduced to writing and carries the signature of both parties to strengthen the commitments made. Contracts should not be coerced and should be entered upon in good faith. This means that both parties truly want the contract to be successful. There is no precise template or model for writing a contract but it should contain certain elements to be complete.

I. <u>Basic information</u>—name of child, names of adults who participated in contract discussions, duration of contract.

II. <u>Overall goal</u>—statement as to the nature of the issue(s) to be addressed.

II. <u>Expectations for child</u>—descriptive and specific statements as to what the child will do and/or will cease doing.

IV. <u>Expectations for parent</u>—descriptive and specific statements as to what the parent will do and/or will cease doing.

V. <u>Monitoring</u>—how and when will contract be monitored for effectiveness; should include a specific date and time that contract performance will be examined.

VI. <u>Declaration</u>—signatures of parent and child, date of contract.

Taking the previous situation of Howard and his mother, let us see what a contract might look like.

Family Contract

<u>Parent/Guardian</u>: Sheila Gold   <u>Child</u>: Howard Gold

<u>Contract Goal</u>: To agree upon a set of rules which will allow Howard more personal freedom and at the same time provide his parents with sufficient information to make sure he is safe and able to be contacted.

(This statement grew out of a discussion between Howard and his mother where both voiced their needs. Effective communication skills, especially "seek to understand before being understood," were employed.)

Expectations for Child:

1. Howard will ask his parents for permission to engage in after school and weekend social activities.

(This was a tough point in discussions. Howard had been doing this but wanted to be set free. His parents were unwilling given Howard's responsibilities at home which are often pre-conditions for his going out; e.g. homework, chores, etc. A parental concession, see below, was needed to gain agreement.)

2. Howard will always call home and cell (leave a message if no one answers) indicating where he is. If the location changes Howard will call with the change either before he leaves the old location or within 15 minutes of arriving at the new location.

3. Unless a parent grants a specific waiver, curfew for school nights is 9:00 and for weekends 12:00 (midnight).

4. Howard does not smoke, drink or use drugs and will continue this pattern. If he feels tempted, he will discuss his feelings at a family meeting.

(This was a tough concession for Howard. He wanted to just be trusted. Although trust is still the basis for this statement his parents were able to have Howard commit to non-use and to recognize that circumstances might prove difficult for Howard to resist if he does not have a specific back-up plan.)

Expectations for Parent:

1. Permission to go out will not be arbitrarily withheld. Reasons for denial will be explained in detail and be related to other family agreements.

(This is the concession that was made to have Howard agree to his first expectation.)

2. Sheila will not remind Howard about what is expected of him.

Monitoring:

1. In two weeks from the date on this contract the status will be discussed at a family meeting.

2. If either side violates this contract, it shall be considered suspended until a new contract can be negotiated.

(This is a consequence provision. Although a specific disciplinary action is not being stated for non-compliance, it is understood that breaking the contract puts the goals and contract terms on the table for re-negotiation.)

Declaration:

This contract represents the product of discussions and agreement between the parties and both parties have entered into the contract in good faith without coercion by either party.

_____   _____

Parent Signature   Child Signature

Date: _____

Several points should be made before leaving the subject of contracts. At times, parents would prefer to have a specific consequence placed in the contract if there is non-compliance. For example, breaking a curfew will result in being grounded the next weekend. If both parties agree, there is nothing terribly wrong with this approach. However, it does create an idea or expectancy that not following the contract is an option. If one believes that there is no excuse for choosing to break a known rule, why create the space for this to happen before the fact. It is preferred that we respond to breaking a contract using The Plan format. This turns the process back to the basic issue of choosing behaviors to meet needs and finding alternatives. In addition, The Plan provision for restitution will focus on responsibility of the child to whoever experienced a loss as a result of breaking the contract. Pre-determined consequences feel more like punishment than discipline. The only exception might be with a child under the age of 7. At that stage of development, a known anticipated consequence is more consistent with the child's level of moral development and could prove useful in the rule setting and contracting processes.

Put Up Or Shut Down

By now many of your are probably saying, "All this process stuff sounds great on paper but in the real world my kid isn't always going to share at meetings, talk about needs and write plans and contracts." The answer is "You're absolutely right." Children will often prefer being scolded or punished to discipline because punishment is quicker and requires less work on their part. They pay their dues and it is over. In addition, they often find ways of negotiating their way out of all or part of the punishment because the parent often meted it out in a moment of anger and realizes that it is excessive or inappropriate.

Parents need a means that is not punishment but will get the child to the point of processing with them. In Family Centered Parenting, "Shut Down" is the recommended procedure. Shut Down means exactly what the words say. The child's world is shut down until they are ready to engage in problem solving. Shut Down can take on different forms depending on the circumstances but the underlying theme remains the same. The matter at hand is of sufficient importance that no other business can go on until it is responded to. It may not mean that the issue must be entirely resolved at the moment but that an interim plan has been put into place until the problem can be dealt with in its entirety.

When, as parents, we are at the point where Shut Down is necessary, several steps should be followed. Shut Down is the only place in Family Centered Parenting when a parent takes complete charge. Because of the adult power position it is essential that this unilateral exercise of power be used with care. If not, we will be modeling behaviors inconsistent with what we are preaching—a certain recipe for failure. First, we must be very clear, in unemotional and direct terms, why Shut Down is being imposed. Next, we must be reasonably certain that we can fulfill what we are attempting to do. For example, if we define Shut Down as being confined to your room we then must be prepared to monitor and takes steps to keep the child in the room. Lastly, we must make it clear under what circumstances Shut Down will end.

I'm sure that some of you might be saying that Shut Down is really the same as the well known practice of "time out." Granted, that although on the surface it might appear the same as time out, the differences lie in presentation and purpose. As indicated, Shut Down is imposed only when a child refuses to engage in problem solving and that must be clearly communicated to the child. Also, Shut Down lasts until the child is ready to engage. It is not exclusion for a specific period of time.

An example might be useful:

Let us suppose that a family meeting has been called and that the children know that one of the issues to be discussed is ground-rules for choosing TV programs. The family has one TV for use by the three children in the family room of the house. Lately there has been much bickering centered around the TV and angry feelings are spilling over to other aspects of family life. At dinner mom mentioned that she is uncomfortable with the arguing and feels that it is contrary to the family mission statement. She says that she plans to place TV viewing on the agenda at Sunday's regular family meeting. On Sunday, when the meeting gets to the TV issue, Wayne, the 11-year-old middle child, says that he does not want to talk about TV watching. Dad turns to Wayne and asks, "How can the three of you come up with mutually agreeable ground rules if you don't participate in the process?" Wayne persists in his refusal. Dad then replies, "Until you participate in the process of making rules for watching TV there can't be any assurance that the arguing will stop. Therefore, you are shut down from TV watching until you are ready to be part of the process. In the meantime, your brother and sister can work on interim ground rules for themselves."

This is a case where a focused Shut Down is appropriate. It is called focused because the Shut Down is limited to the specific issue that is causing the problem. It is also important to note that the parents carefully adhered to the recommended Shut Down procedures. There was a clear communication of the problem stated in "I" statements by mom. An established family procedure, the family meeting, was suggested as means to deal with the issue. However, Wayne refused to engage in the process and was reminded that it would not be possible to engage in an activity that is causing a problem until the problem is resolved. This is the point where adult action is used to curtail the power and freedom of the child and must be accompanied by a clear explanation to the child. Dad also leaves the door open for problem solving and establishes the conditions under which the Shut Down will end.

Earlier, a situation between Howard and his mother Sheila was presented. Let us go back there to further illustrate the Shut Down process. Let's imagine that when Sheila confronted Howard about the telephone call from Aunt Phyllis,

Howard said that he didn't want to talk about it. This would be another situation calling for a focused Shut Down.

The logical response for Sheila would be, "Howard, as a parent I am morally and legally responsible to make sure that you are safe. Until you are able to discuss what happened and what the future will look like regarding rules for going out the only way I can meet my needs as a parent is to make sure you don't go out. Therefore, until this issue is resolved you have chosen not to leave the house except for school and other scheduled obligations. The ball is in your court. Let me know when you are ready to talk."

Examining Sheila's responses we can see that most importantly she controlled her emotions. She could have easily lost it and told him he was grounded for two weeks and walked out. Although this would be a fairly natural consequence for his behavior, it would not address the underlying issue and would probably create even more tension between parent and child which most likely will manifest itself in some other form of negative behavior down the road. As we have discussed, when parents overpower their children the consequence is a power and freedom reduction in the child. This in turn leads the child to additional behaviors, which are often inappropriate, to regain the lost power and freedom. Sheila used "I" messages to establish her standing in the issue. Standing, as previously mentioned, is the justification for intervention and is especially crucial to articulate when a parent is using power for Shut Down. Sheila was clear in letting Howard know what her parental needs were and that the only way to satisfy them was to shut Howard done until he was willing to engage in a problem solving process that would be need fulfilling to both parties. The other issue that Sheila had to have considered was her ability to enforce the Shut Down. Apparently Sheila is certain that she can monitor Howard's compliance. Shut Down must be enforceable to have its desired effect. Lastly, Sheila informs Howard what he has to do to end the Shut Down and that it is ultimately his choice to be restricted. Again, the use of the word choice preserves some power for Howard and gives him the space to end the Shut Down.

At times, parents may have to impose a broad-based Shut Down. This means that the child's life is virtually on hold until they are ready to engage in the problem solving process.

As an illustration, consider Margie and her mother, Ann:

Margie is a 15-year-old high school freshman who has been extremely moody of late. Although not atypical adolescent behavior, it has gotten to the point of rudeness to her mother. Margie barks orders at her mother, complains when things aren't done right away, and when reminded of family rules regarding her demeanor to her mother, she responds with sarcasm and a "Whatever." Ann again reminds Margie that she finds her behavior personally disturbing and that she would like to sit down with Margie and figure out what is going on. Margie says she is too busy to talk and goes to her room and shuts the door. Ann goes to her room and knocks on the door. Margie says, "I don't have time to talk, leave me alone." Ann replies, "I do not feel good about myself when I am being treated in a manner that I find disrespectful. I want to deal with this issue so that I can continue to relate to you in a way that allows me to feel comfortable. Therefore, until you choose to take the time to engage in a problem solving discussion with me your life is on hold. Other than going to school or scheduled non-social commitments, I will not drive you anywhere, prepare meals for you, nor permit you to watch TV, use the telephone or Internet unless you prove that it is for school business." Ann leaves Margie's room.

This is obviously a broad-based Shut Down since it does not focus on halting a particular behavior but restricts almost all of the child's actions. The reason is that Ann's concern is not restricted to a specific kind of event but rather it relates a more generalized set of behaviors. The logic for the Shut Down is that Margie's communication style and attitude is preventing any interaction necessary for Margie to get what she wants from her mother. Therefore, until corrected, Ann can no longer respond to Margie. Again, following the guidelines for Shut Down the parent(s) must be clear about their standing in the issue and articulate this to the child in "I" statements. Ann did this quite clearly, without losing her temper, when she defined her own diminished power by virtue of her daughter's rudeness. Ann then communicated that Margie had a choice to make and that she was ready to problem solve with her. Lastly, we must assume that Ann can follow through with the outlined conditions of the Shut Down.

Shut Down can take on many forms depending on the age of the child, the ability of the parent(s) to enforce the restrictions and the logistics involved. At times shutting down will inconvenience the adults and we must make sure that the child does not gain power by doing so.

An illustration should help:

Angela, a seven year old, is on her way to the supermarket with her mother, Lucy. Lucy has had problems with Angela's behavior in the supermarket. Angela gets bored easily and then starts making demands on Lucy to buy things. Angela also starts to complain about how long it is taking to shop. In anticipation, Lucy discusses with Angela on the way to the market what are the appropriate behaviors in the market and Angela appears to understand. In the midst of shopping Angela begins her antics. She starts asking for things and complains loudly. Lucy has a choice. She can ignore Angela and deal with the problem later or she can act now. Given the fact that Angela did know the expectations for her behavior and that she has acted this way before, Lucy decides to go further and she stops shopping.

She tells Angela that it is too distracting to shop and they must go home. In essence Lucy has shut down the shopping process. At home, Lucy tells Angela that they will have to do a plan on what happened. If Angela refuses, then a broad-based Shut Down is imposed. However, once planning begins it is essential that the planning process take into account the inconvenience and loss of Lucy's time in having to go back to the supermarket. For Angela, stopping her mother from shopping is empowering. She has used negative behaviors to prevent her mother from doing what was needed. Therefore, The Plan must both address both Angela's power needs and a provision to make restitution for Lucy's loss of time. This could include not taking Lucy to a future event (party, visit to a friend) in order for Angela to gain time make up for what she lost by having to return to the market.

As indicated, Shut Down can take on a number of forms and is either specific (focused) or broad based. Regardless of the manner, it is an essential tool for a parent to exercise in order to orient a child to the positive, need fulfilling practice of problem solving. However, since the Family Centered Parenting process is based on a foundation of empowering without overpowering, parents should be cautious and thoughtful about using Shut Downs in a way that they become punishments rather than a component of the discipline process.

ACTIVITY #4-1— FOR *each one of your children, design what a broad based "Shut Down" might look like in your family. Your response should include what resources (time, manpower, etc.,) will be needed to make the shutdown effective.*

A working copy of this and all activities can be found at
www.GrowingGreatRelationships.com

In conclusion, it is obvious that putting Family Centered Parenting practices in place requires considerable thoughtfulness and energy. Hopefully, the many examples presented in the chapter will provide the guidelines for parental decision making that empowers both parties and fosters harmonious family life.

Growing Pains—Cultivating The Mission

By now it should be clear that adopting Family Centered Parenting practices will involve a number of transitions in the life of your family that in the short run won't be painless. The age of the children and the degree a family is already implementing procedures similar to the Family Centered Parenting strategies will determine how smoothly the transition progresses. The long term prospect is that Family Centered Parenting will provide a family life that is positively need satisfying for all family members, increases the joy of raising children and also builds a foundation for creating and maintaining life-long relationships between parent and child.

Established habits and patterns of family life don't change easily. According to needs theory, these behaviors are the best choices individuals have made to meet their needs at a given point in time. As we have discussed, these choices often have undesired consequences and are at the root of our negative emotions (anger, anxiety, depression). In other words, even if there is a lot of unpleasantness going on in the family, the status quo is an attempt to be need fulfilling. Therefore, things have to get pretty bad before individuals will be willing to give up current habits for new ones.

As an illustration, consider a child who repeatedly avoids doing his household chore of taking out the garbage. His parents punish him with a partial loss of allowance or denial of TV privileges. After the punishment things are all right for a few days but then he reverts to his old ways. Several things are going on. The punishments are indeed losses but he has become accustomed to them.

Furthermore, he has no reason to think about the reasons for not doing the chore. In addition, something about not doing the chore, despite consequences, is need fulfilling. The status quo has now evolved into a pattern of inconsistent fulfillment of responsibilities, parental disapproval, punishment and no change in the overall pattern. Disrupting the status quo by adopting Family Centered Parenting practices will require an initial investment of extra time and energy by parents. Since punishment is quicker, a child will most likely resist having to examine his behavior and to commit to a plan for change. One should readily expect that initially a Shut Down experience would be needed to get a child to choose to engage in problem solving his/her issue.

As parents we often experience the dissatisfaction with the status quo before our children. We might have an image of a harmonious family in our minds, either as a result of our own growing up or an ideal we have set for ourselves. Our children might have never experienced or imagined this possibility. Their reality is the day to day life of the current family. Therefore, a parent will most likely be the proponent of change before the children. If this is the case, and it often is, there will be resistance and suspicion about implementing Family Centered Parenting.

An example should be helpful.

The Canterino family consists of the mother, Delores, the father, Frank, and two children, Marie, age 9, and Robert, age 12. Both mom and dad work outside the home but Frank works longer hours and has been putting in a lot of overtime lately. The children attend a school based after-care program and Delores picks them up on her way home from work. As soon as they get in the car Robert & Marie start verbally abusing each other. It usually starts with mild teasing then quickly escalates into insults and shouting. Delores is often worn out and frazzled from her day at work and her patience is limited. She yells at Robert and Marie and tells them to shut up. They arrive home start to argue about using the computer and begin to nag mom about getting dinner ready. Delores begins to prepare dinner (Frank usually eats later when he gets home) and attempts to stop the kids from bickering by threatening to shut off the computer. At dinner, Marie buries her head in a book while Robert devours the baseball stats in the newspaper. Delores asks the kids about how their day was in school and is received with a conversation ending response of "fine." The children finish dinner and another dispute breaks out about whose turn it is to clear the table. This is the last straw for Delores. She screams at the kids and threatens them with no TV if the table doesn't get cleared. Amid the mutual put-downs the children complete the chore and leave the kitchen. When Frank gets home, Delores tells him how unhappy she is with how things are going with the family. Frank says that things seem pretty normal to him and tells her she is just overtired. Delores remembers reading about Family Centered Parenting and suggests that they have a family meeting. Frank reacts with skepticism but says he will agree. Delores tells the children that they are going to have a family meeting on Sunday morning after church. Robert and Marie say that it is a "dumb" idea and that there is nothing to talk about. Besides, they both made plans to go to a friend's house after church.

All but one member of the Canterino family is locked into the status quo. Understand, that except for Delores, the family members are attempting to meet their needs and know no other path ways to achieve those needs that would yield a more satisfying and enriching environment. The children maintain their connectivity (love & belonging need) to each other and to their mother through the ritual of an argument followed by a grudgingly offered concession. This behavior is also rewarded by attention from the parent. The argument/concession cycle prolongs interaction with the parent thereby affording additional recognition (power) and control of time (freedom) to the child. Dad looks to work and his role as provider to fulfill his need for power but may be using his heavy work schedule to avoid a non-fulfilling family situation. As a result Delores remains as the only family member expressing dissonance (discrepancy) between an image of what family life should be and the reality they are experiencing on a daily basis. The status quo is need fulfilling for three of the four members of the family. Delores has to take the initiative for change. The expectation is that once they get involved in Family Centered Parenting they will discover patterns of behavior that are far more need fulfilling and satisfying than the status-quo.

To break the deadlock, Delores will have to be very aggressive about articulating her needs and her unhappiness to the family. Using "I" statements she has to insist that the family commit to at least exploring the Family Centered Parenting process by participating in several family meetings and drafting a family mission statement. It might even be necessary for Delores to initiate her own self Shut Down to reinforce her conviction that the Canterino family has to change the way it operates. A suggested presentation by Delores to her family might sound like this:

"I must tell all of you how I feel lately. I am unhappy and frustrated in my role as a mother. The way we communicate with each other, with frequent arguments and threats, is personally very upsetting. I don't feel our love, caring and support for each other coming through. I would like to see this family as place where we all feel connected to each other in a close and positive way. I see our family as a kind of sanctuary from the hardships of life and a place to get the energy to face the challenges life presents. I am committed to doing what is necessary to work with you to make this happen. How about it?"

Delores' presentation has many effective elements. It is brief and direct. She opens with a strong statement about her own needs as a mother. She gives an example of what is bothering her without using words like always or never. She reinforces her message with a positive by assuming that the underlying strength of the family is there. This creates the needed gap (discrepancy) between what is and the picture she paints of what it should be. She concludes with her personal commitment and an invitation for the family to participate.

If Delores does not get the cooperation of her family she would have to raise the stakes and be prepared to engage in a personal Shut Down. This could take the form of a statement as follows:

"As I told you last _____, I am not feeling fulfilled in my role as a mother nor am I satisfied with our family life. Since there does not seem to be a desire to explore this matter as a family, I have chosen to shut myself down and not continue doing things as I have in the past. I will not provide transportation beyond picking you up at school. I will not prepare meals for the entire family and I will not participate in any family outings. Although this is not what I want, at least it will spare me the frustration of doing what I do and feeling no satisfaction. At such time as this family can commit to discussing and working on these issues I will again actively participate in family life."

This is a powerful statement from Delores. However, it may be the only way to bring change to the Canterino family system. Delores uses "I" statements to express her needs and uses the word "chosen" to make it clear that she is taking responsibility for her own behavior and not blaming anyone else. She also indicates under what conditions she will change her behavior. In essence we have a self-imposed Shut Down by a parent in order to break the status quo.

It is safe to say that implementing Family Centered Parenting will require persistence and patience but that the rewards will far outweigh the effort needed to bring about change. Clearly, those families with relatively young children will have an easier time because the status quo is not yet entrenched. Logically, therefore, families with teenagers will likely experience the greatest resistance to change. In these families patterns and habits are well established. On the other hand, older children do have additional life experiences to bring to the table. Furthermore, the conflicts surrounding the management of teenagers in of itself are often of sufficient magnitude to alter the status quo. This creates the opportunity for change and the creation of new systems within the family.

An additional potential difficulty can come from close friends or relatives. Grandparents and older aunts and uncles often have fairly rigid approaches to child rearing. Although these relatives might have a great deal of wisdom, their ideal picture of child rearing and appropriate behavior might be far different from yours. These folks are often well meaning but their suggestions imply criticism of what you are doing. A common comment might go something like, "If you would be just a little more strict with _____ I know s/he would do better." It is important that you respond without defensiveness and remember the principles of effective communication. If you feel the individual questioning your approach is sincere, you should be comfortable in explaining what the process is and asking them to withhold judgment until Family Centered Parenting has had a chance to work. Consider inviting a relative to a family meeting to see for himself or herself. This inclusionary approach can be highly need fulfilling (love & belonging) for the relative. Another suggestion is to get together with a small group of parents who are also adopting the Family Centered Parenting practices. The mutual support and exchange of ideas can help parents get through the tough period when the status quo is being challenged. In addition, this helps parents meet their own needs for connecting to others. In the long run your commitment to Family Centered Parenting will silence the naysayers. It is obvious to outsiders when a family is in harmony. This speaks volumes to its own success in a powerful way.

Chapter 5

LIVING AND BREATHING: FCP TAKES ON YOUR WORLD

Because of its core principles of building responsibility and valuing the specific needs of individuals and families the Family Centered Parenting is designed to accommodate a variety of unique family characteristics. However, it would be helpful to focus specifically on how the Family Centered Parenting approach responds to life's challenges.

Hot Topics

Parents are naturally greatly concerned about issues that affect the safety and welfare of their children. High-risk behaviors such as substance abuse and promiscuity certainly top the list. Our information age culture certainly serves to exacerbate the normal anxiety parents experience in their attempt to protect their children from the excesses of behavior that they are constantly exposed to in the media and in the community. Although we associate these behaviors with adolescence, it is unwise to wait for adolescence before we begin to discuss these issues within our families. As mentioned earlier, prevention involves preparing our children for the choices they will have to make far in advance of the time they will actually have to make those choices.

The first part of prevention or being proactive is to accept the reality that our kids are going to make choices about their behaviors. Despite government efforts to win the "War on Drugs," a substantial number of middle school and most high school students in our communities know where to buy drugs. In fact, in some areas it is harder to buy alcohol or tobacco than illegal drugs. Therefore, the majority of children by the time they are 13 years old will be in a situation where they have to decide whether or not to experiment with drugs, alcohol and tobacco. These decisions will be made in the company of their peers without close adult supervision. This places total reliance on a child's decision making abilities. Clearly, one or two discussions or a parental threat is not sufficient training to our prepare our children for the tough choices they must make. The Family Centered Parenting approach, both as a process and as a philosophy, can be extremely powerful in our preventative interventions with our children.

The family meeting provides an excellent forum for on-going dialogue and information sharing surrounding the hot topics. As a family evolves and shares issues and concerns, discussions naturally turn to the challenges that both children and parents face as the children grow older and are learning how to spread their wings. Parents have the responsibility for making sure that the family meeting agenda covers those matters that are of the highest concern by prompting discussion with simulations of problem solving situations that their children are likely to face. The meeting also provides a safe place for children to share their feelings about the choices they are confronting or will confront. This clarifying of feelings and attitudes is the best preparation we can give our children for facing the tough decisions they will have to make.

The Family Centered Parenting philosophical link to basic needs theory provides parents and children with the framework for hot topic discussions. Beyond pointing out the obvious consequences of high-risk behaviors, it helps parents and children understand that people choose behaviors, which might seem to be self-destructive because those behaviors are an attempt to meet a basic need. The best way to avoid those behaviors is to find an alternate behavior that is less damaging yet still need satisfying. Substance abuse is based on a need for fun. Many individuals choose getting high on drugs and/or alcohol in order to find a short cut for getting their fun needs met. The family meeting is the appropriate place to define the need for fun and to discuss the ways we can get our need for fun met that do not put as at risk for addiction and illegal activities.

Responding to peer influence, an important ingredient in high-risk behaviors, can be framed as an attempt to meet one's need for love and belonging. Adolescents are particularly vulnerable to peer approval and dread being singled out. Therefore, they will often decide to go along with the crowd, rather than isolating themselves, even when they are well aware that a behavior is inappropriate. At the family meeting the need for love and belonging is analyzed as it pertains to peer influence. Children are given the opportunity to articulate the many ways they can meet their love and belonging needs without risking social ostracism or indulging in high-risk behavior.

Sexuality and the behavioral choices young people face regarding physical intimacy should also be an important family meeting topic. Again, by using needs theory as a starting point, children can understand how their need for love and belonging influences their behavioral choices regarding intimacy. For most parents, especially with the detailed sex education curriculum offered in schools, their role shifts from information provider to values clarifier. This is the more difficult challenge and certainly well suited to the family meeting environment. Family meetings naturally adjust to the maturational level of the children. As children mature, the topics increase in complexity because they are part of an on-going process of discussion rather than an arbitrary time for the "sex talk."

It should be noted that what makes the "hot topics" tough on parents is often their own ambiguous feelings about the subjects. Parents who enjoy a glass of wine with dinner or an evening cocktail wrestle with the issue of behaviors they are modeling for their children. A large number of parents, especially those who came of age in the 70's, experimented with recreational drugs and experienced the excesses of the sexual revolution. Now, as parents, they must reconcile their past behaviors with the values they feel are important to model and transmit to their children. Family Centered Parenting gives parents a context for analyzing and comparing their own past behavior with the messages they want to transmit to their children. Understanding our needs as adults and the choices we make helps us prepare for the questions of our children.

For illustration, consider the discussion in the Wilson family:

Carl Wilson and his wife, Anita, were college students in the late seventies. They did their share of partying and met while they were both attending graduate school. They married and have two children, Wendy, age 14, and Kyle, age 12. Both Carl and Anita work outside the home and live a fairly mainstream suburban lifestyle. They are relatively new to Family Centered Parenting and have been holding family meetings for the last several months. Given the age of their children, they are anxious to bring up the topic of drugs with them. In anticipation of some tough questions, Carl and Anita start a dialogue on how to handle the subject. Both of them do not want to lie to their children but have differing points of view on how to handle the inevitable question, "Mom, Dad, did you ever smoke marijuana when you were a teenager?" Carl is inclined to tell a version of the truth, to the effect of yes we did experiment but found it not that great and we learned from our mistake. Anita, feeling very uneasy and more than a little ashamed would rather dodge the question with an answer such as it really doesn't matter what I did 25 years ago. Carl and Anita, after several discussions and Internet research, began to frame the issue from a needs theory perspective. Anita realized that her embarrassment stemmed from her power need in the form of needing to be viewed by her children as a "perfect" mother. Admitting that she had experimented with drugs would detract from her image as being a good mother. Carl saw the issue from the perspective of modeling that one could make mistakes but grow from them. Admitting a shortcoming and demonstrating the strength to overcome it would enhance his power as a father. They agreed that meeting their needs for fun and freedom had influenced their earlier behaviors and this might be helpful in the discussion with the kids. Ultimately, Carl and Anita agreed that their answer to the children would be, "What does the question have to do with your decision making regarding drugs?" To them, this response preserved their integrity since they were not going to lie to the children while it shifted the conversation back to the issue of their children's need and behavioral choices.

This example was not intended to give the single "best" answer for the tough questions children are likely to ask, but rather to model a process for thinking ahead and being clear about one's needs as a parent. Family Centered Parenting is only the road map for getting to a destination that the parents have decided that they want to reach.

In general, keep in mind that being a role model does not equate with perfection. In order for us to be truly authentic to our children we do have to acknowledge that we make mistakes. Someone, with great wisdom, said that we only fail when we do not learn from our mistakes. Our children will make mistakes and errors in judgment. How they respond and what they learn from them is the true mark of character. Therefore, as role models we serve our children well when we can honestly deal with our own shortcomings.

Schooling

Issues and decisions surrounding education and schooling consume much of the time and energy in our families. The process of Family Centered Parenting provides the framework for preparing the family to make decisions and solve the inevitable problems that result from the educational experience. Although not specifically part of Family Centered Parenting, it would be remiss not to make some overall observations of what the research suggests as practices which enhance our children's progress in school.

Research data is emerging that demonstrates a connection between specific parenting practices and a student's academic success. There are what has been defined as "parental engagement behaviors" which lead to greater student learning. The main focus is parental engagement at home. Not surprising, the evidence strongly suggests that the home environment is among the most important influences on academic performance.

Four types of parental engagement at home have been identified. They are: actively organizing and monitoring the child's time; helping with homework; discussing school matters with the child and, an activity particularly beneficial for younger children, reading to and being read to by children. Since each of these areas should be addressed within the context of individual families' unique circumstances there is no single recipe for how it should be done. Certainly the family meeting and problem solving process incorporated in Family Centered Parenting is an important tool for fostering these behaviors.

If we examine the first type of engagement—actively organizing and monitoring a child's time—in more detail, the strategies to accomplish this will become clearer. Children need routines to thrive. This is especially important in our fast-paced, overloaded world. Typically, arranging schedules among the demands of lessons, sports, religious instruction and parental work responsibilities is an awesome challenge. Even arranging our children's play time becomes complicated in most communities where children have to be driven to every activity. Investing the time and energy to plan and coordinate these activities in order to meet everyone's needs is essential. Be mindful, however, that this doesn't mean parents are expected to do this alone. If they do, they will be diminishing their children's personal responsibility and taking on the role of "Super Parent." Family meetings are a good forum for setting up the schedules, calendars and methods of communication to make sure that it is all working. The inevitable conflicts that arise will be minimized with careful planning. In addition, by utilizing a portion of meeting time for this task we are reinforcing the message that the family is in this together while simultaneously providing a forum for any family member to voice his/her stress or unhappiness about the expectations being held for their behavior by other members of the family.

The second principle of engagement—helping with homework—needs elaboration. Homework offers an opportunity for parents to show an interest and to take a direct role in their youngster's schooling. Here the degree of involvement is important to define. To begin with, homework parameters need to be discussed and agreed upon in the family meeting. Questions about timing, location in the house and acceptable parental monitoring should be answered with agreement reached by the members of the family. The line between assisting with homework or teaching the material is a fine one. It is certainly acceptable to point out an error or to offer an explanation for something that your child hasn't mastered. However, if s/he really doesn't understand the bulk of the assignment then the teacher should be contacted. Parents should be cautious about micro-managing homework and instead should devote their efforts to taking a leadership role in creating family systems which monitor and oversee but do not restrict individual choice and responsibility for achievement.

The third principle of engagement—discussing school matters with your children—is second nature to those families practicing Family Centered Parenting because discussion is a core value in the life of the family. A key ingredient is being a good listener and questioner. A question such as, "Tell me about your day in school." is sufficiently open ended to elicit the good and the bad and is far more productive than, "How was school today?" The former invites dialogue while the latter often leads to one-word responses. Follow up questions help clarify the magnitude of an issue and demonstrate that you were listening. When a problem materializes such as being bullied by a peer or being ignored by a teacher, the parent has to decide when to intervene. Sometimes, especially when children enter the middle school grades, they claim to be able to handle the problem themselves because they fear being embarrassed in front of their peers when a parent comes to school. It is critical to establish some standard of whether or not they can truly handle the problem alone. If the agreed upon standard is not met then the parent must intervene.

The fourth principle—reading to and being read to by your child—is foundational for literacy skills. Children who are read to build their vocabularies and learn the syntax of their native language in the most natural way. It is also a time for closeness with your child and serves to model the importance and joy taken in reading. As children mature, the practice can be shifted to having the child, at times, read to the parent. Not only does this continue to reinforce language skills but also provides the child with a feeling of mastery as they share their reading skills with a parent. Being read to and round-robin reading aloud by family members is a wonderful family tradition that can be carried on into the teenage years.

Another dimension of being engaged is how you manage your involvement with your child's school and teacher(s). Attending school performances and fund raisers is important but not nearly as crucial as your interaction with teachers. In the elementary school grades, teachers seem to expect a great deal of involvement from parents, usually on the teacher's terms. Most schools hold scheduled teacher conferences early in the school year in addition to the open house presentation. The scheduled conference follows the teacher's agenda. Therefore, it is important for a parent to prepare their own questions and voice their concerns. You can also be assured that if there is significant problem with your child, you will hear from the teacher. Remember that no one really knows your child better than you and you need to share what is unique about your child. It is also a good idea to contact your teacher for a follow up conference even when there is nothing particular going wrong. It sends a message that you are an involved parent, and your expectations for the teacher are high. You want to make sure your child is being challenged and that his/her individual strengths and needs are being met in the classroom. Staying involved with teachers becomes more problematic as your child advances in the grades. Part of the issue is the onset of adolescence. As children mature and begin to define their identity separate from parents

Being an engaged parent is need satisfying for all parties. It gives parents a level of control essential to feeling worth as a parent while children feel loved and acknowledged for what is happening in school, the place where they spend so much of their time.

Fathering

One could argue that there should be no need for a section on fathering. Parenting is parenting and the gender of the parent should make little difference in this task. After all, the Family Centered Parenting approach is based on the principle that all human beings have the same basic needs with no distinctions made for age or sex. On the other hand, our personal definition of how well these needs are being met—quality world picture—is unique for every individual and clearly shaped by gender. Some combination of biology and evolving cultural expectations related to gender roles do provide us with standards as to the degree our needs are being met as males or females. The degree that biology determines, beyond the obvious physical characteristics, how men and women parent is certainly subject to hot debate.

From a cultural perspective, the parenting norms among men and women are easier to understand. In most cultures mothers have historically tended to spend much of their time, while also attending to other responsibilities, on day to day childcare especially in the early childhood years. For women, for the most part, their power needs as defined as being a "good parent" are met when they are able to nurture at a level deemed appropriate by the expectations shaped by their social reference group. Except for a few bumps in history, women have been validated as parents in traditional nurturing roles. Men, on the other hand, have been validated for their prowess as hunters, protectors—the male expression of nurturing—and providers as well as being responsible for bringing boys into adulthood.

Teaching the rituals of manhood to adolescent boys is a remarkably consistent practice in ancient cultures and still observed today in the few remaining aboriginal groups. As human activity became more diversified, these rituals evolved into fathers teaching sons how to farm or how to learn the skills that they had mastered as artisans. Even when a boy was apprenticed to someone other than his father, it was to an older male who taught him his craft. It is only since the beginning of the Industrial Revolution (about 200 years ago) that a father's role has shifted so dramatically. Although a father continued in his role as the primary provider he became far less present for day to day protecting and teaching. However, despite changing roles, men with children still seek to have a portion of their power needs met by being perceived as good fathers. Unfortunately, for many men, this has become focused entirely on providing. In modern society this means working at a job away from the family. Men, therefore, have become increasingly isolated from the routines of family life with the results being that they feel validated only as sperm donors and as check writers.

This narrowing of the source of validation has created a number of consequences for men and their families. Frequently men abandon their families entirely when their ability to earn has been curtailed. Rather than remain in the home, without sufficient validation as a provider and its resultant negative impact on a man's need for power, men have sought other ways to prove their worth often in a manner that is harmful to themselves or others. Additionally, as men become increasingly involved in their worklife away from home, there is little left to contribute to the day to day life of the family.

The consequences of this emotional rather than physical abandonment of the family are considerable. For example, recent research has shown that teenagers who don't get along with their fathers in two-parent families are more likely to smoke, drink and use drugs than those raised by single mothers. According to a recent report by the National Center on Addiction and Substance Abuse at Columbia University, children raised by their mother alone were 30 percent more likely to use drugs than those living in supportive two-parent homes. But those children with two parents who have poor relationships with their father have a

68 percent greater risk. The study found that mothers influence their children's important decisions three times as often as fathers do and are more likely to have private talks about drugs.

Beyond the obvious increased risks of substance abuse, there are other more subtle consequences of emotional abandonment by fathers. Fathers do things a little bit differently with their children than mothers. This special parenting style is not only highly complementary to what mothers do but is by all indication important in its own right for optimum child rearing. For example, studies have shown that fathers play differently with their children than mothers. A father's play behavior tends to be more physically stimulating and exciting. It tends to challenge a child's physical and mental skills while emphasizing risk taking and independence while mothers focus more on emotional security and personal safety. Both styles are important and underscore a clear message that becoming a mature and competent adult involves the integration of two somewhat contradictory human needs—power expressed as independence/individuality and love and belonging expressed as connectedness. Fathers tend to focus on the former while mothers on the later. When a father removes himself from the family either physically or emotionally, important components of raising healthy children fall solely to the mother thereby stretching her ability to take on roles that are better suited for an involved father.

The challenge for men is to redefine their quality world picture of how they satisfy their needs as fathers. This is especially true for the way men fulfill their roles as protectors. As mentioned, protection in our modern world is very different than in the past. The job of protector was easier to define when our predators were four legged or members of an invading tribe. The threats to our children's well being are far more subtle and removed and require a different skill set to protect the family. Instead of brute strength or accuracy with a weapon, fathers must orient themselves to teaching responsible decision making, problem solving and independent thinking. To be good at it men must be especially mindful of those effective communication techniques that promote listening and two-way conversation. Men have a tendency to problem solve before validating feelings and this can substantially impair their ability to coach their children. Utilizing the Family Centered Parenting approach, fathers can better fulfill their roles in ways that are truly need satisfying to them and to their families. As Gail Sheehy writes' "They (men) are discovering a secret that women have always known: The easiest way to feel loved and needed and ten feet tall is to be an involved parent." (New Passages, page 281).

Blended Families

Blended families are certainly becoming far more common in our 21st century society. By definition, a blended family is one where two parents join together in one household each having primary custody of one or more children. In these families there are many issues that must be addressed concerning roles, responsibilities, rules and relationships. The biggest issues in blended situations usually revolve around the authority of the stepparent and the relationship between stepsiblings.

Stepchildren are often unsure about the balance of power in the family. There is often a presumption that the birth parent is in charge and that the stepparent is secondary. This might be the case and is not necessarily wrong. In these cases, it is best for the step-parent not to be the disciplinarian but to see himself/herself more as a friend and mentor. However, the key is letting the children know how the adult authority roles will play out. Again, there is no precise formula for making these decisions and individual family needs will certainly define the available options. For example, the presence of non-custodial biological parents in the lives of the children will certainly be an important factor. If a child maintains a close relationship with a non-custodial birth parent then clearly the potential confusion for the child regarding the roles of biological parent and stepparent increases. For example, a younger child might call or refer to a stepfather as "Daddy" when speaking to his/her birth father. This can provoke an angry or resentful response from the biological father, which is highly unsettling for a child. Children need guidance and support in order to achieve the resilience necessary to successfully manage their way through the blending process. Therefore, it is strongly suggested that Family Centered Parenting practices be adopted **before** the families merge.

Creating a mission statement for the new family is a good place to start. This process will not only promote connectivity (love & belonging) but will also establish the importance of proactive communication as a means to anticipate and solve family problems. Furthermore, it sends a clear message that the new family is a value-based entity that must meet the needs of all the participants. The family meeting format should be used to put on the table the concerns of all members of the new family as decisions unfold. Children will often focus on logistical matters, which might seem fairly routine for adults but are anxiety producing for children. Blending families often requires a physical move for one or both sets of children. The moving experience itself, regardless of blending, is highly stressful. Children need to know that they will be secure in a new environment and they need to be able to give voice to their fears so that they can be adequately addressed.

As in all families, the meeting should become the venue for voicing and responding to the numerous issues that the family confronts. However, since a blended family is created rather abruptly, the trust among family members that evolves naturally over time in a non-blended family is not initially present. This places an extra burden on the adults to make sure that the meeting becomes a safe environment where confidentiality is respected. This is especially true among the stepsiblings. Sharing private information about a stepbrother or sister with friends may be used as a means to gain power for a child anxious about his/her role in a blended household. Ground rules concerning privacy of family matters should be particularly stressed in the blended family.

Single Parent Families

As divorce rates have climbed single parent families have become far more common in our modern society. It is difficult enough for two parents to raise children; however, when one parent becomes solely or principally responsible for child rearing, there is additional stress placed on the family system. From the routine of providing transportation to the resolution of school or other problems, the single parent must face these demands without the help of a partner. Consequently, there is a tendency for a single parent to either overvalue efficiency or adopt a laissez faire approach to parenting. It is certainly understandable that these may be legitimate responses to being overwhelmed but either extreme compromises effective parenting. As discussed earlier, the need for efficiency can lead to a parenting style that relies too heavily on parental power. This often results in over use of punishment and an under use of more need fulfilling problem solving. The laissez faire approach avoids the abuses of parental power but at a heavy cost—the loss of a family structure founded on shared values shaped by adult experience. In addition, the degree of involvement of the non-custodial parent can also increase the stress on the child and custodial parent. Infrequent visitation or a non-custodial parent who is overtly angry with his/her ex-spouse leaves a child in a vulnerable and confusing emotional place. Ignoring or glossing over this reality can only lead to behaviors which are inappropriate or dysfunctional as the child seeks to meet his/her needs.

Recognizing the less efficient, at least in the short run, nature of Family Centered Parenting, it takes a strong commitment on the part of the single parent to engage in its practices. However, the long term harmony that comes to the family involved in the Family Centered Parenting process will ultimately minimize the stress of single parenting and enhance the lives of both parent and child.

For illustration let us consider the Harris family:

Agnes Harris has been divorced from her husband Harry for three years. They were married 12 years and had two children Mike and Jennifer. Mike is now 12 years old and his sister is 10. Although they have what is legally defined as joint custody, Agnes is the primary custodial parent. Harry has visitation on Wednesday nights and alternate weekends. Agnes and the children remained in the family home while Harry found an apartment about 20 minutes away. For the most part Agnes and Harry communicate via e-mail. Telephone contact is limited to immediate issues such as being late to pick up the kids. In the past, Harry has been pretty good about following the visitation schedule. However, in the last few months he has canceled on at least three occasions. He canceled on Sunday and the kids were disappointed. On Monday, in the car, Agnes overheard them whispering that Daddy was probably hanging out with his girlfriend. In the past week Agnes has noticed that Jennifer and Mike have not been themselves. They seemed distracted and moody. When Agnes asked if there was something wrong they said everything was fine. On Tuesday night Agnes returned home from her aerobics class and found the kids watching a "R" rated movie on HBO. She had told them that they are not permitted to watch "R" movies and that she would cancel HBO if she found them breaking the rule. When confronted, Jennifer said that their father let them watch anything they wanted when they visited him. Agnes was enraged. She turned off the TV set and sent the kids to their rooms. As they left she heard Mike mutter something about wanting to live with his father.

Agnes and the children are at a critical point. It appears that the non-custodial parent might be making some changes in his life-style that is affecting the children yet Agnes has no control over the situation. The children have started to play one parent against the other regarding household rules. Clearly there is much to discuss but Agnes has not yet created the space for this to take place. Asking the children at dinner if something is wrong is not sufficient. The family meeting process would certainly be helpful to the Harris family and it is not too late to start. Agnes will have to take the initiative and schedule the meeting. If she meets with resistance it might be necessary to invoke Shut Down. There is much for Agnes and the children to discuss. A mission statement for the three of them is the logical starting place. Mom can bring up her feelings of powerlessness when she sees her children unhappy because of an action taken by her former husband. She can also ask, initially as a hypothetical, how they would feel if either one of their parents entered into a relationship and even re-married. Also, for immediate resolution, rules for the house should be discussed and the issue of conflicts between Dad's rules and what is agreed upon for the primary home should be dealt with.

Chapter 6

ABOVE AND BEYOND: RESPONDING TO THE UNEXPECTED

As parents, there are times when circumstances beyond our control can make demands on the family which seem insurmountable. The unique needs of a child's disability, mental illness, behavioral disorder or even special talents places enormous stress on the family system. Family Centered Parenting, with some specific accommodations, can offer parents and children the understanding and the knowledge to respond to the unexpected in a manner that keeps the family strong and empowered.

Child With Special Needs

A family with a child with a disability is worthy of attention as a special family situation. The literature reports that approximately 80% of marriages where there is a child with a disability (physical, cognitive, emotional) in the family end in divorce. This alarming statistic speaks to the extra stress on the family of parenting a child with a disability. It seems that every aspect of parenting presents a greater challenge in a family with a child with special needs. Needs theory provides a good framework for understanding the problem and dealing with the consequences in a way that not only helps the family cope but also allows it to thrive.

The most difficult aspect of parenting a child with a disability is the acceptance by the parents of its full meaning. Depending on the severity of the disability, this can be a long journey that requires time and patience. The path to acceptance is not smooth and predictable. There are hills to climb often followed by plateaus of acceptance. The journey to fully accept may seem to be at an end when another life event arises to challenge this belief. The resilience to keep on going is not easy to develop and the lack of it contributes to the breakdown of the family.

Understanding how a parent's need for power—defined as control over one's environment and self worth—can be initially diminished by accepting the disability provides insight into the difficulty of the situation. A disability is a result of an event or circumstance that we usually can't control. Genetic abnormalities, birth traumas, accidents and illnesses are the main causes of a disability and they seem to occur on a random basis. The randomness reminds us of the fact that we do not control significant parts of our destinies and this realization depletes our sense of power. As one seeks to understand why a tragedy happened we might choose blame and anger as behaviors in an attempt to compensate for the loss of perceived power. Our partners are often the targets. In our need to make sense of the situation—restore power—we might blame his/her gene pool, her risky behaviors during pregnancy or the "should haves" that might have prevented the accident. Obviously these behaviors directed inwardly in the form of guilt or outwardly directed at partners can stress a relationship to the breaking point.

Our self-worth as adults and parents is, to some extent, also related to the accomplishments of our children. This is natural since self-worth is at least partially based on what others think of us. When our children achieve, it reflects positively on our parenting and the personal characteristics that we have passed on to our children. Hence, telling others what our children have accomplished fulfills our need for power. Although this tendency can be excessive in some people—we all have probably experienced an acquaintance or relative who goes on and on about what his/her children have achieved—it is an exaggeration of normal boasting rather than unnatural behavior. Parents of children with disabilities, at times, feel that they have little to be proud of. Parents of a child who uses a wheelchair know that they will not be able to cheer their son on at the high school football game nor dream of their daughter winning a field hockey scholarship. Parents of a child with a developmental disability cannot hope to see their child go to an Ivy League college. This imagery of loss has the potential of being devastating to one's internal quality world picture of being a powerful parent. The results of these perceptions vary and are not only self-destructive but also severely impact on the well being of the family.

Men will often distance themselves from the family both physically and emotionally. The perception of not being powerful as a parent will lead them to a search for power outside of the home either by becoming a workaholic or over investing in a fraternal, sporting or community activity. Women may over invest as nurturers or caregivers of their child with a disability. This can result in a loss of self and excessive dependency by the child on the parent. Regardless of the form it takes, unless a parent's internal picture of being a powerful parent is modified by the constraints of their child's disability, they will be choosing behaviors that are intended to increase power but will ultimately lead them on a negative path. Successful changing of our internal picture is what leads on the path to acceptance.

Family Centered Parenting gives families the tools for working through these issues. The family meeting, beginning with the creation of a mission statement, is a family's primary methodology. Formulating and modifying the family mission statement serves as the foundation for the family to define itself. This definition, by its very nature, brings the issue of disability to the forefront. The mission statement allows a family to give voice to its uniqueness. For the family with a child with a disability its vision, quite naturally, weaves the disability into the fabric of the family. In other words instead of being a family with a disabled child, the vision is of a family with value based interdependencies where the focus is placed on the individuality of each family member, not just on the special needs of the child with a disability.

The mission statement of a family with an individual with special needs should not be remarkably different from any other family. The core values and practices—respect and support, need fulfillment, living in harmony—which families typically incorporate into their mission statements are universal. The differences among mission statements are usually more reflections of style rather than substance because the greatest value in constructing a mission statement lies in the process of creating the statement and in the on-going comparison of the mission with family behavior.

A fundamental part of the family meeting process is for each member to explore how his/her needs are being met. This emphasis is especially critical for the family with perceptions of loss because of a member with a disability. A safe environment is crucial in order for parents and children to talk frankly about the perceived shadows that are lingering but not acknowledged due to shame. Parents have to put on the table that their need for power as parents is partially dependent on the accomplishments of their children and that the disability seems to make their ideal internal picture out of reach. This admission, although painful, sets the stage for a re-orientation of their quality world picture. In reality, achievement is not based on an absolute standard but rather on accomplishment of a goal where standards are based on relative starting and ending points.

For example, for a child with dyslexia learning how to compensate sufficiently to read on grade level is just as great or greater an accomplishment as a child without special needs making high honor roll. When parents start to feel that sense of pride that comes with achieving a goal, independent of markers imposed on them by others, they will find their need for power being satisfied. Is it any less joyful for a parent and siblings to cheer a child competing in a wheelchair basketball league than on their high school basketball team?

The re-orientation of quality world pictures is clearly just as important for all members of the family as for the parents. However, because of their status as role models, parental leadership by example is essential. When parents are able to re-frame their indicators of success and pride, the children learn the vocabulary and define their power needs in new ways. Family meeting discussions of setting goals and creating game plans for meeting those goals which reflect the challenges presented by a disability serves to put into operation the behaviors that lead to the desired match between ideal world pictures and real world actions.

Without doubt, the key to the success of the family with a child with a disability in general and for that child in particular is the degree of self-worth of the child. When acceptance takes hold and power is no longer sought from angry and blaming behaviors, one is on the path for building a strong sense of self-based on self-efficacy—the ability to accomplish goals. The family unit supports the search to formulate goals and as a resource to meet them. As obstacles materialize, the family serves as the place to voice misgivings and disappointments and to help adjust game plans to overcome the difficulties. Because of the sharing, the accomplishments and sense of power accrues not only to the individual but also to the family as a whole. This is especially important for the siblings of the child with a disability who often feel that undo attention is being directed towards the child with the disability. The shadow for siblings is the guilt they feel for resenting the time and energy focused on their brother or sister with a disability. They need a safe place for expressing the resentment and help in understanding that the resentment is an attempt to regain power lost by perceived parental inattention. Empowering the child without a disability through ownership in the successes of their sibling with a disability helps to diminish the resentment.

Parental needs for fun and love and belonging may also be more difficult to meet in the presence of the disability. The extra care needed to meet everyday responsibilities can be sufficiently time consuming and energy draining to leave little time for relaxation and socialization outside of the family unit. It is important for parents to acknowledge these needs and to actively work to meet them. Support groups within the disability community are quite helpful in this area. Friendships with families facing similar issues serve as both a resource for new ideas and as a means for validating the challenges that are being confronted. These groups usually have access to the latest information on the disability and what new resources are available to make life a little easier for all concerned. Control (power) increases as we gain knowledge about the disability while love and belonging is satisfied through new social interactions.

Child With Exceptional Gifts & Talents

Parenting a child who has been labeled as gifted or talented academically, artistically or athletically can be a mixed blessing. On one hand, as parents, we bask in the knowledge that our child is "exceptional" and has abilities that are being recognized that are above and beyond the average child. On the other hand, in order for these talents to be nurtured and developed, it can require a considerable amount of time, money and disruption in family routines. In addition, the "non-gifted" child or children in the family will often feel that their needs are being deferred because of the special sibling.

Clearly what is required is for the Family Centered Parenting model to be followed with little deviation. The gifted child, by definition, has unique needs that are beyond the capabilities of standard resources. Schools should offer some additional programming for academically gifted students in order to hold their interest but implementation is spotty. Neighborhood music and art schools are usually not sufficiently sophisticated to respond to the needs of a talented musician or artist. School sports teams and local recreational leagues may or may not have sufficient challenging programs for exceptional athletes. It is obvious that the fact finding alone for resolving these issues is time consuming and stressful. The tough part comes from the choices that need to be made and the consequences for the family of those choices.

Again, the family meeting and the family vision become helpful tools to navigate the decision making and its consequences. The vision serves as the framework for defining the family's values concerning the nurturing of talents. For example, after several family meetings a family with one or more children who are exceptional might adopt a mission statement which includes the following phrase:

The _____ family will at all times work together to develop and support the unique talents of all members of the family.

This rather simple statement contains a very powerful message and serves as a blueprint for future decision making. By agreeing to "work together" the family is committing to act as a team and to share in the success of each member of the family. Additionally, by indicating "unique talents of all members" the child with the exceptional ability is not singled out. There is an accepted understanding that we all have the ability to develop our talents and that although one member's support might require more resources and time, the underlying value is that each member of the family will have the opportunity to develop his/her talents.

The family meeting process serves as the forum for planning and implementing the strategies needed to fulfill the family mission. The myriad details needed to manage the needs of the exceptional child—practices, competitions, travel to events—can best be worked out when the family works together, listens to each other and agrees on plans that take into account everyone's needs.

Challenging Behaviors

Oppositional Defiant Disorder (ODD)

All children are oppositional from time to time, particularly when tired, hungry, stressed or upset. They may argue, talk back, disobey, and defy parents, teachers, and other adults. Oppositional behavior is often a normal part of development for two to three year olds and early adolescents. However, openly uncooperative and hostile behavior becomes a serious concern when it is so frequent and consistent that it stands out when compared with other children of the same age and developmental level and when it affects the child's social, family, and academic life.

In children with Oppositional Defiant Disorder (ODD), there is an ongoing pattern of uncooperative, defiant, and hostile behavior toward authority figures that seriously interferes with the youngster's day to day functioning. Symptoms of ODD may include:

- frequent temper tantrums
- excessive arguing with adults

- active defiance and refusal to comply with adult requests and rules

- deliberate attempts to annoy or upset people

- blaming others for his or her mistakes or misbehavior

- often being touchy or easily annoyed by others

- frequent anger and resentment

- mean and hateful talking when upset

- seeking revenge

The symptoms are usually seen in multiple settings, but may be more noticeable at home or at school. Five to fifteen percent of all school age children have ODD. The causes of ODD are unknown; however, if we look at the behavior from the perspective of need fulfillment it might provide insight for how we respond to an ODD child.

Opposition, Anger & Need Fulfillment

As indicated in earlier chapters, in order to change or modify a behavior it is important to understand what need is being met for the child by that behavior and that our responses might actually be reinforcing the very behavior we need to stop. This seems particularly difficult with oppositional behaviors because, to those impacted by the behavior, it is difficult to imagine that these extreme behaviors can in any way be need satisfying to the child. However, if we step back and look closely at the impact on the environment by oppositional behaviors we can gain considerable insight as to the need fulfillment aspects of those behaviors.

When an individual is oppositional the world takes notice. It is hard to ignore loud vocal outbursts laced with profanity and threats or acts of physical aggression towards people or property. The more outrageous the behavior the more aggressively we respond. Often that response, out of our frustration, starts to look a little like the very behavior that we are reacting to. One might reasonably ask, "What could possibly be need fulfilling about a child's tantrum and a parent's angry and punishing response?" If we look at the effect this behavior has on the environment we can see that the child is now in control. The life of the family has become focused on the ODD child. Caregivers must ignore everything else and focus entirely on the child's outrageous behavior. In addition, the adults in charge are now clearly upset and reacting with emotion. Adding to the mix might be angry responses from siblings who were targets of the oppositional behavior. It should be clear that the child has gained an enormous amount of control over his environment and this directly feeds his need for power. Power, as defined in the first chapter as one's influence over his/her environment, is flowing to the child by virtue of the disruption caused and the subsequent attention received by his/her extreme behaviors. The child who gets adults emotionally reacting to him acquires even more power. In addition, the child who is now in an angry state is feeling powerful in his/her anger. Since anger is everyone's quick fix to restore their feeling of power it should be evident that an oppositional child is additionally fueled by working himself into an angry state. An ODD child has learned that his/her oppositional behaviors gives him/her an instant and strong dose of power. In a sense, a child has become addicted to getting power by virtue of his anger.

Caregiver Response

Reduce Resistance—If we follow the fundamental principle of Judo that redirecting an opponent's force, off-balancing the opponent rather than simply putting up resistance, several strategies become clear. The strategies are intended to reduce the disruptive impact of the child's behavior thereby limiting the amount of power the child derives from being oppositional.

Ignore—Choose your battles and do not react to the small stuff. If a child's behavior is negative but not really doing harm other than inconvenience do not reward that behavior with your attention.

For example:

A child going to his room is verbally belligerent about having to go to bed. S/ he might be yelling, cursing and or protesting. The first reaction from caregivers might be to confront the child about this inappropriate verbal behavior which will only escalate the child. Instead, as long as the child is going to his room, do not empower the negativity with attention. Simply ignore it.

Control Your Emotions—It is essential for the caregiver of an ODD Child to have control over his/her emotions (see Chapter 2, rule #5). The ODD child perceives adult upset and emotional reaction as an empowering sign that they are controlling the adult's behavior. That means no yelling, threats, hitting or other physical signal that you are upset. Verbal responses should be in a well controlled tone that is clear and direct. Offer choices and make sure that your body language is also not threatening. Over time, non-verbal reminders (signals) can be negotiated with the child so that s/he can receive a quick reminder that a particular behavior must stop. This step is especially crucial to a child who is also diagnosed with ADHD.

Avoid No—The word "no" and its equivalents, often triggers an oppositional episode. The oppositional child interprets a command to halt a behavior as an indicator that the particular behavior will disrupt the environment and earn him even more attention. The alternative to "no" is the question to the child, "What are you doing?" The expectation is that the child can identify the inappropriate behavior and make a value judgment as to the negative aspect of the behavior. This technique is much easier to implement if rules have been developed with the child before an incident occurs. Using the family meeting strategy (see Chapter 3), to negotiate rules that are owned by the child will make this type of intervention possible.

For Example:

Tony often pushes or punches his younger sister. Typically, his mother yells at him to stop and Tony justifies his behavior by saying his sister took something from him. Tony and mom scream at each other and she punishes him by sending to his room and taking away TV time. However, this strategy doesn't seem to be helping.

The following alternative approach is based on the assumption that at a family meeting the rule that children in the family never physically harm each other has been agreed to.

Tony is watching TV with his sister, Maria, in the living room. Mom hears Maria crying and she runs into the living room. Maria says that Tony punched her and pushed her off the couch. Mom asks Tony in an emotionally neutral fashion the following questions:

1. *What did you do?*
2. *Was your behavior consistent with our rules?*
3. *What need were you fulfilling by this behavior choice?*
4. *What are the consequences for meeting your need this way?*
5. *What will you do to make things right with your sister?*
6. *How can you meet your need in a way that is within our rules?*

If Tony refuses to discuss the issue, then follow "shut-down" procedures (see Chapter 4) until Tony is ready to talk.

Long Term Strategy

If we accept the premise that an ODD child has learned to fulfill his/her need for power through oppositional behaviors it is essential for the child to be able to meet the need for power in a more appropriate and sustaining manner. In the long run this will gradually reduce oppositional behavior as the child meets his needs for power through positive alternatives. Usually children have their power need met by being successful in school, through athletic accomplishments, and by praise for responsible behavior at home. However, by the time a child is already exhibiting ODD behaviors many of the appropriate means to fulfilling power have been limited by the ODD itself. Therefore, a vicious cycle has been created whereby the ODD prevents power from being derived through acceptable behaviors and the child then relies more on the ODD behaviors which further limit getting power appropriately. Applying the indicated strategies consistently along with help from school personnel is necessary to begin to break the cycle and shift behavioral choices from oppositional to more appropriate power fulfilling behaviors.

Tips

1. Structure situations to insure success and offer generous praise and other incentives when success is met.
    a. avoid known difficult environments
    b. rehearse rules and strategies before engaging in an activity.

2. Catch a child doing the appropriate thing. Even if it is baby step heap praise upon any success the child might achieve.
    a. reward progress towards a goal not just for meeting the goal.

3. Help your child become good at something. Find an activity or skill that your child can become highly competent. This will raise their social standing and earn recognition (power) for their accomplishments.

   a. individual sports/activities (swimming, martial arts, music, art, crafts)

   b. collecting

   c. sports or music trivia

4. Work closely with school personnel and make sure your child has an Individualized Educational Plan (IEP) that recognizes his/her ODD and specific effective strategies in school to respond to those behaviors.

5. If your child also has been diagnosed with ADHD (not uncommon for both conditions to exist at the same time), make sure that this is being treated with medication combined with counseling.

6. When your child is in rage mode dialogue or discussion is not possible. Isolate your child for up to 20 minutes to allow stress hormones for child and parent to subside.

7. Whenever possible offer choices when giving directions. Choosing is empowering and reduces the chances of a child saying no to a directive.

8. Educate friends and relatives who come into contact with your child about ODD and the strategies you are using to deal with this disorder.

ADHD

Many parents who are having difficulty with parenting either have been told or suspect that their child has Attention Deficit Hyperactivity Disorder (ADHD).

To respond appropriately it is of primary importance to be as certain as possible that the child truly has this disorder. Establishing a diagnosis of ADHD depends on a comprehensive evaluation of the child with input from multiple sources such as parents or caregivers, teachers and physicians.

Reports of core symptoms of ADHD directly obtained from parents (including the age of onset, duration of symptoms and degree of functional impairment) and assessment of the child for associated or coexisting conditions are required. The American Academy of Pediatrics has published a Clinical Practice Guideline for the diagnosis and evaluation of the child with ADHD. This publication states that the diagnosis of ADHD requires that a child meet Diagnostic and Statistical Manual of the American Psychiatric Association, Fourth Edition (DSM IV) criteria.

The DSM IV criteria for diagnosing ADHD require that symptoms of inattention and/or hyperactivity-impulsivity have persisted for at least six months and that they are more frequent and severe than typically observed in individuals at a comparable level of development.

Some symptoms of ADHD must have been present before age 7, with some present in at least two settings (home and school). There must also be clear evidence of the symptoms affecting social or academic functioning. While most children with ADHD have symptoms of both inattention and hyperactivity-impulsivity, one symptom pattern may predominate. This can result in three different possible subtypes. Hyperactive-impulsive type which is the rarest, predominantly inattentive which is more common in girls than boys, or the combined type (inattentive plus hyperactive-impulsive) which is the most frequently diagnosed.

Once a child is properly diagnosed the best treatment consists of a combination of medication and behavior therapy. The psycho-stimulant family of drugs (Ritalin, Adderall and their generic equivalents) are somewhat to highly effective with about 80% of those children who are properly diagnosed with the disorder.

At home, Family Centered Parenting strategies are generally highly effective with children with ADHD but require some modifications. The core element of Family Centered Parenting, the family meeting process, remains as a foundation for the entire family to understand and to learn how to respond to the demands of the child with ADHD. General information concerning the disorder must be shared with all family members. It is critical that the behaviors which characterize ADHD are understood to be the product of the disorder not a result of willfulness or a character flaw. This can only happen when information is shared and discussed within the family. The knowledge gained is an important ingredient in building tolerance and patience with the ADHD behaviors by the other members of the family. Another benefit of the family meeting for the ADHD child is the acceptance and support from the family, which can be expressed and demonstrated during meetings. Since there is no cure for ADHD, the best way for a person with ADHD to function successfully is to learn how the disorder impacts his/her functioning and, most importantly, to learn how to compensate for its effects. The motivation to do so flows from a feeling of self-worth. The empowerment gained by recognition and understanding supplies the energy to learn compensatory strategies with the family becoming a significant source of this energy. The specific modifications are more centered on techniques than changing the basic Family Centered Parenting strategy.

Psychology of ADHD

ADHD impairs the development of normal **inhibition** thereby creating a cascade of secondary difficulties throughout our executive system. The term "<u>dis-inhibition</u>" serves as a functional description of the ADHD individual. The chart below describes the major impairments in functioning for an individual with

ADHD

IMPAIRED FUNCTION	CONSEQUENCE	EXAMPLE
Diminished sense of time	Nine-year-old Jeff routinely forgets inability to hold events in mind; defective hindsight; defective forethought	Important responsibilities such as deadlines for book reports or after school team practice are missed
Internalization of self-directed speech	Deficient rule-governed behavior; poor self-guidance and self-questioning	Five-year-old Audrey talks too much and cannot silently give herself useful directions on how to perform a task
Self-regulation of mood, motivation and level of arousal	Displays all emotions publicly; cannot censor them, diminished self-regulation of drive and motivation	Eight-year-old Adam cannot maintain persistent effort to read a story appropriate for his age level and is quick to display his anger when frustrated by assigned school work
Reconstitution (ability to break down observed assignment behaviors into component parts that can be recombined)	Limited ability to analyze behaviors and synthesize new behaviors; inability to solve problems	Fourteen-year-old Ben stops doing a homework assignment when he realizes that he has only two of the five assigned questions; he does not think of a way to solve the problem such as calling a friend to get the other three questions

Strategies for Managing ADHD in the Home

Principle—*Externalize what is deficient internally to achieve behavior management objectives.*

Key Words—*Relationship, Brevity, Variety, Structure*

Relationship

Research on the neurological relationship between emotion and learning reinforces the principle that we need to create an environment that provides both physical and psychological safety for children to maximize the cognitive energy available for learning. Since building rapport is easier with a younger child, the parents of adolescents must be especially mindful of strategies to build a relationship with their child.

Brevity

ADHD causes low productivity for all tasks. Therefore, attention and concentration are greatest in short activities. Frequent, brief activities covering chunks of information/activity will result in greater outcomes.

Variety

Children with ADHD tend to perform more poorly on the second presentation of a task because they are hindered by their "flagging attention." The ADHD child who perceives an activity as repetitive or boring will have difficulty staying on task. Presenting directions and information in novel ways or with different applications can maximize attention. A parent should see him/herself as a performer.

Structure

A consistent routine enhanced by a highly organized format to activities will provide a focused environment for an easily distracted child. Specific daily schedules that include well-planned experiences with smooth, well-defined transitions from one task to another are optimal. Rules, expectations and consequences should be clearly stated and be highly specific.

Tips

1. Insist on eye contact.

2. It is easier to go from structured to unstructured; therefore, careful planning is necessary when transitioning from an unstructured activity.

   a. younger children—use auditory or visual cues to signal changes in the routine or breaking points in the activity.

   b. older children—use a visual cue

   c. other transition options include: brief conversation revisiting an earlier activity, limited physical chore (set table, pick up a toy)

   d. set and examine the home schedule and coordinate structured activities with transition activities

3. Capitalize on the ADHD child's need for visual information by offering frequent visual cues as you present information.

   a. use an erasable board to offer visual explanations that supplement verbal descriptions

      1) draw webs or maps

      2) highlight material using color to emphasize special points or areas

      3) number things that are presented to help a child locate the correct place

4. A child with ADHD rarely gets all verbal material presented. At times they may repeat verbal information immediately after hearing, but the next day they have little integration of thought. When presenting complex or multi-step directions include the following elements:

    a. use key phrases to maintain attention and focus children on the steps in the directions (one, two, three, wash up, focus, this is the next step)

    b. use numbers or letters of the alphabet to sequence the steps of a verbal direction just as you would with written instructions.

       (1. find your toys on the floor 2. small toys in the red box 3. stuffed animals on the bed)

    c. reinforce a verbal message with an animated style and visual supports

5. Low productivity, completing tasks, and planning tasks effectively, are usually more of an issue than a weakness in skills unless there is a diagnosed learning disability. ADHD children benefit from a parent posting a daily schedule and reviewing it frequently. The schedule can be written each day on the erasable board. Colors and shapes to designated different activities are useful.

    a. schedules should include time frames for each activity

    b. cross out each completed activity as it is accomplished

    c. shorten tasks

    d. avoid timed activities

6. Visual modeling and role-playing help ADHD children recall instructions and directions. Children are highly reinforced by peer models.

    a. when rules or procedures are introduced, have a sibling act out or actually do the beginning steps of the process

    b.   parents may act out or role play things such as the proper way to perform a task

7. Color is highly effective in drawing attention to relevant discriminative stimuli. Color can help to enhance but take care not to distract.

    a.   add color accents to key features of repetitive tasks that childrenfind un-motivating

    b.   highlight areas on written materials where multiple directions make the activity more complex

8. Excessive motor responses such as fidgeting should not be handled as a disciplinary issue. Ignore when possible.

    a.   encourage a child to hold a rubber ball or other squeezable object

    b.   redirect by handing the child an appropriate object or movement to a constructive task

    c.   model less distracting motoric responses

9. ADHD children often appear to be "daydreaming."

    a.   provide activities that require active participation

    b.   encourage visualization as a rehearsal technique

    c.   allow children to doodle while listening to directions

    d.   use a mechanical timer to reinforce the time restraints of an activity

    e.   variety and success are antidotes to inattention

10. ADHD children often have difficulty with remembering.

    a.   use mnemonic strategies to cue recall (pick a familiar word where the each letter corresponds to a particular task or action—see the example below).

       *Use the word **FASTER** either orally or written on a chart when a child comes home from school and needs to start homework. **F** = find* your work in your backpack, **A** = *arrange the materials you need,* **S** = *start the work,* **T** = *take your time, don't rush,* **E** = *examine for mistakes,* **R** = *replace homework in backpack*

   b.   encourage the child to repeat instructions back after they are given

   c.   color code significant details

   d.   teach visualization techniques

11. Behavior intervention strategies must be carefully planned and implemented consistently with ADHD children. Behavior modification is helpful because it focuses on the external with students who manifest little internal control.

   a.   have children participate in developing home/family rules and make sure those rules are displayed visually in a prominent place in the home (creates ownership)

   b.   rewards must be **frequent, salient and non-distracting**

      (1) catch child doing something right

      (2) token economy—points traded for food, cash or trinkets

      (3) set realistic behavioral objectives as standards for rewards (use baseline data as standard for improvement)

      (4) non-verbal rewards such as touch and signals

   c.   behavior charts prominently displayed with frequent updates as to standing in the system (record points after each designated time block)

   d.   allow children to listen to a MP3 device while working on individual tasks

   e.   set behavioral expectation before each activity

   f.   choose carefully in which areas you are seeking compliance to rules and procedures (Don't sweat the small stuff!)

12. Parents must be proactive about the social skills issues presented by their ADHD children and the reaction of their non-disabled siblings and peers to inappropriate social behaviors.

    a. hold family meetings to discuss issues before they become problems and utilize them as a format for problem resolution

    b. find a formal social skills group which focuses on transferring learnings to actual situations

    c. find and enhance a skill or hobby that a child is interested in so that they can raise their "social currency" with peers

    d. prior to a social situation (family event) rehearse rules and expectations in a non-threatening manner

Chapter 7

WHAT ABOUT???
FREQUENTLY
ASKED QUESTIONS

I n the course of working with parents on Family Centered Parenting, these issues have arisen with sufficient frequency to be addressed directly.

What should I do if my spouse is not in agreement with the Family Centered Parenting process?

In a number of families the primary caretaker, often the mother, is more likely seeking to find a better way of dealing with parenting issues. The spouse with fewer day- to-day parenting responsibilities may be avoiding the issue by absenting him/herself or living in denial. Therefore, one parent is seeking change while the other is removing him/herself from the process. The first approach would be to ask the reluctant partner if they are satisfied with the status quo? If the answer is no, than the response should be an invitation to try something different and see if it brings results. A contract, not necessarily in writing, should be created between the parents which indicates that the reluctant parent will make an effort to support the Family Centered Parenting process for a specified period of time and then discuss the results. If the answer to the original question is yes, than the dissatisfied parent has to clearly express the frustration s/he is experiencing and ask the spouse for support while changes are made. The parent looking for change must rely on the relationship with his/her partner and ask for cooperation to at least attempt the new approach.

At times one parent, again more commonly the father, will accept the fact that changes need to be made but finds Family Centered Parenting inconsistent with his beliefs about child rearing. This is most likely the result of an authoritarian upbringing. Couples caught in this dilemma often argue about methods of disciplining with mom being more process oriented and dad more punishment oriented. Men who are caught up in this problem often accuse their wives of being too soft on the kids and insist that if they were tougher things would be better. Whether he is aware of it or not, the father probably subscribes to the Theory X view of human nature. Therefore, the first approach would be to ask him to read the first chapter of the book. If he is still fixed in his beliefs then he must be asked to allow change to take place on a trial basis for a specific time period. At the conclusion of the agreed upon interval the results will be discussed. This approach requires a relationship between husband and wife strong enough for one party to ask the other to try something new for the sake of the other party even if they do not agree with what is being asked of them.

Why is Family Centered Parenting a better approach for dealing with the hot topics like substance abuse and sexuality?

Most experts in substance abuse prevention and sexuality education indicate that talking to our children is the best means of dealing with the issues. Since verbal communication is so intrinsic to the Family Centered Parenting process both in family meetings and in problem solving, the family following the approach has created a comfort zone for discussion. This comfort zone becomes a safe space, for both parent and child, to talk about topics that are controversial and awkward. Parents often struggle with finding the "right time" to talk about the hot topics and consequently wait until an issue arises. This is too late for the purposes of prevention. In Family Centered Parenting the non-problem solving family meetings are excellent forums for prevention and information type discussions. Furthermore, in these meetings simulation experiences, where children can explore techniques for responding to situations outside the family, can be practiced.

As children enter the vulnerable pre-adolescent and adolescent years, parentally imposed limitations on behavior become increasingly significant issues. Teenagers are developing their individuality and are often attracted to forbidden behaviors to demonstrate their separation from parents. Clearly communicated family values which children have had a stake in creating are a parent's best defense against self-destructive behaviors. The Family Centered Parenting process stresses the creation and refinement of values and rules through dialogue and mutual respect. Again, experts in the field of substance abuse prevention report that children who have an inner sense of family values, which they can rely upon in situations where they might be tempted to experiment, are better able to make responsible decisions. Family Centered Parenting is based upon creating this inner voice.

Lastly, Choice Theory, the foundation of Family Centered Parenting, provides an excellent framework for understanding why people abuse alcohol and drugs and engage in promiscuous behaviors. Children can understand at a remarkably early age that substance abuse is a misguided attempt to satisfy the need for fun. Promiscuous behaviors are often attempts to satisfy the need for love and belonging. Also, high-risk behaviors in general are frequently ways adolescents seek to have their growing need for freedom fulfilled. Needs theory gives the parent and child a common vocabulary for interpreting behavior thereby facilitating a process for responsible decision making.

How can Family Centered Parenting help us counter the negative impact family on our family of media influences such as violence, sexual excess, under age drinking and smoking?

First, it is important to be clear that the jury is no longer out on the issue of media influence. The most recent studies have linked aggressive behaviors with exposure to violent video games and violent content on TV and in movies. Simply put, the kids who are exposed to the most violence are more likely to act aggressively. Furthermore, children who watch "R" rated movies with the greatest frequency where cigarette smoking, alcohol abuse and sexual content is prevalent, are more likely to indulge in these behaviors than children who do not watch or rarely watch these movies. Most adults did not need these studies to make the connection between viewing and behavior. Humans learn most behaviors by imitation. Therefore, what children see they tend to repeat. However, despite this knowledge many parents have been reluctant to take significant action on the subject. It is important to understand their hesitation.

Parents do not want their children to be so isolated from peer culture that it interferes with their ability to make friends. We want, quite reasonably, our children to fit in socially. For example, if a group of 12-year-old girls are talking about an episode of a popular TV show and you did not permit your child to watch the show because of its sexual content, your daughter could very well feel left out. In order for your daughter to respond and feel good about herself, she must be able to explain to her friends why her family has a rule concerning TV viewing. This is a difficult task and can only be accomplished if she understands the rule and was a participant in its formulation. Family Centered Parenting requires participation in rule setting and an understanding why a particular rule is needed. Even if the child does not fully embrace the rationale behind the rule, if they were full participants in the rule setting then they, with less fear of rejection, will be able to articulate the reasons for the rule to peers.

As an example:

Imagine Rita, a seventh grader, talking to several girls at the table in the school cafeteria. The girls are talking about a movie that was on HBO the night before. They ask Rita what she thought about it. Rita replies, "It was an R rated movie with explicit language and graphic violence. We have a family rule that none of us will watch this type of movie." One should note several features of Rita's response, which are results of Family Centered Parenting. Rita's statement that, "We have a family rule….." utilizes the word "we." This serves to communicate that the rule was not imposed upon her and that she was a stakeholder in formulating the rule. Rita is sufficiently empowered to give an honest answer rather than lie to fit in with her friends. Furthermore, her indication that none of the members of the family watches the movie sends a message that she is from a family with shared convictions. Friends might question her about her statement. This would be to her advantage because the clarity of her answer will communicate important information about her individuality and the strength of her family. Without family meetings, where parents willingly share the reasons for their beliefs and children get to express themselves and contribute, Rita would be far more vulnerable to compromise her values for the sake of conformity.

In the Rita example, it should also be noted that the rule about watching this type of movie applied to the whole family, not just the children. One can assume that in the course of the discussion about this rule, Rita probably questioned why it was all right for adults to watch gratuitous violence and not children. Not having a good answer, the parents were then morally obligated to join in and make it a family rule. This type of discussion and decision is integral to the Family Centered Parenting process.

Another approach to dealing with the influence of media is to be present with your children when they are exposed to it. Clearly, parents can probably be fairly effective in controlling their children's exposure to certain cable TV shows or "R" rated videos, yet between the evening news and what is now considered "family" entertainment on broadcast TV, much of what children view is provocative in nature. Our only defense against a media message that is contrary to our family's values is to be there to comment, explain and dialogue over what is being presented. For example, if a character in a sitcom is indulging in pre-marital sex or having an extramarital relationship, after the show we can ask our children what they think the consequences of this behavior might be for the characters. In other words, we use the content of the show as object lessons for a broader discussion of values, rules and consequences. This not only reinforces the values of the family but also fosters critical thinking and sound decision making skills in our children.

What guidance does Family Centered Parenting provide concerning household chores and allowance?

Family Centered Parenting does not provide pat answers for these topics but does offer a process for dealing with them that is need satisfying and uniquely suited to the circumstances of a particular family situation. Again, the family meeting should be viewed as an opportunity to put these issues on the discussion table as a means of preventing conflicts and disagreements.

The driving force in the family meetings regarding chores and allowance should be the values held by the parents which will shape the values of the children. As mentioned, the earlier in the life of the family that Family Centered Parenting begins the more influence parents will have in helping to shape values. It is less stressful to assist in shaping our children's values than to impose new values on top of ones that might already have been influenced by the environment outside of the family.

The dialogue on chores and allowance should begin with a discussion over the beliefs held by the participants and the origins of those beliefs. Parents might come to the understanding that some of their attitudes are based on what they did when they were children rather than formed by reflection upon their beliefs and goals for their children and expectations of the quality of family life.

Since a fundamental principle of Family Centered Parenting is creating ownership in the well being of the family, it seems logical that families would naturally come to the conclusion that sharing household responsibilities would further that objective. Discussing each family member's capabilities and likes and dislikes regarding chores is a good starting point. This type of discussion permits family members to talk about their unique needs while reinforcing the all-important concept of behavior being need fulfilling. In addition, by focusing on the consequences to the entire family of not doing a chore, the idea of responsibility to the family as a core value is also reinforced.

The practice of dispensing allowance either as payment for chores or given independent of chores is a helpful means for developing fiscal management skills in our children. There is nothing like a child spending money on a frivolous item only to have nothing left for something they really need or want to serve as a natural consequence for not managing money. Although there is no pat rule for deciding whether or not allowance should be tied to performance of chores, parents should keep in mind that doing chores is meant to contribute to the overall maintenance of the family and should be seen as a means of reinforcing ownership. Therefore, payment for chores might be seen as contradictory to this perspective. Furthermore, the reinforcement provided by accomplishing something useful for the benefit of the family is internal and far more powerful than the reinforcement of an external reinforcer like money.

Regardless of the particular details of chores and allowance practiced by a particular family, the most significant part of the issue is really the process used by the family to monitor and adjust the details through dialogue at family meetings. As the family matures, needs and capabilities change and a forum should always be available to revisit the subject and negotiate changes as needed.

Does talking about the mistakes I make
and have made in my life weaken me
as an authority figure to my children?

This question speaks to the core issue of modeling. That is acting in a manner we wish our children to act. On one hand, as role models for children, parents want to present themselves as being pretty terrific people. When children look up to us it meets our needs for love and belonging. When children are obedient and follow parental advice the adult's need for power is met. We associate these interactions with highly positive words like respect and admiration. However, sometimes being on a pedestal can be a precarious place. We might want to mask our frailties in order to preserve our image of perfection. The fear that our children might lose respect for us if we admit weakness can lead to a loss of ourselves and a model that our children just might perceive as unattainable. A child who feels s/he can never equal his/her perfect parent loses self-esteem and will often give up trying. This is the downside of being the perfect role model. This is especially true for younger children who tend to aggrandize the power of adults in general and their parents in particular.

Adolescents by the very nature of this stage of development are far more prone to question the capabilities and judgment of parents. Parents with adolescents who are dealing with the "hot topics" are especially vulnerable to questions about what they did when they were teenagers. As long as it isn't overdone, most parents find that their children enjoy hearing stories about what it was like when they grew up. Consequently, our children want to know how we handled the challenges of personal freedom, partying and dating. The challenge is to respond in a way that is authentic and validates the concern of the child without giving them the message that since their parents pushed the envelope and wound up alright, they too can indulge in these behaviors. Below are some suggested ways to respond. However, remember that the parental response should be sincere and be the product of some adult reflection about our true beliefs and values on these topics. Teenagers have a good sense of what is "real" to them and if we sound too perfect or preachy they will shut us off.

➢ *What I did and the mistakes that I made should not be an excuse for your decision making.*

➢ *The legal consequences for some of the behaviors I indulged in were not as severe as they are today. (especially true for possession of controlled substances)*

➢ *A lot more is known today about the physical harm done to our bodies due to tobacco, alcohol, and drugs.*

➢ *The consequences of unprotected sexual activity can be deadly.*

➢ *If I knew then what I know now I would have behaved differently.*

➢ *The price I paid for my excesses were ....*

➢ *What we really must focus on is how to get your needs for freedom and fun met with few negative consequences.*

The other side of the coin is the parent who constantly gives voice to his/her own shortcomings. Either through blaming others and/or themselves for things not working out as planned they model a victim or helpless role. This extreme can create a sense of anxiety in a child. The message they receive from the helpless parent is that the world is a scary place with little ability to control what is happening in life.

The middle ground is what we should be striving for. Our children need, for their sense of well being, to experience their parents as sufficiently masterful to create a safe place for them. Young children, as mentioned, will naturally view their parents as powerful figures so we really don't have to stretch the issue with excessive self-praise. However, children do need to develop resiliency—the ability to bounce back from adversity. We learn how to be resilient through modeling and experience. Parents who acknowledge an error or problem then take responsibility for its solution are demonstrating resilience to their children. They have not attempted to hold the impossible standard of perfection as an indicator of self-worth but have modeled the reality that things do go wrong and mistakes happen. The key is not indulging in self-pity and, after acknowledging the fact that something has gone wrong, acting in a way to make things better.

A related issue is how we deal with our mistakes when it specifically regards an action we took with our children.

An illustration might be useful.

Martha came home from work at her usual 6:00 p.m. time only to find that her 12 year-old-son Ron was not at home. There is a standing rule in the family that if Ron is playing at a friend's house after school he is to be home by 6:00. Martha is annoyed and starting to get a bit worried about Ron. At 6:30 she starts calling Ron's friends. On the fourth call she reaches his friend Wayne's mother. She says that Ron is with Wayne and they are working on something in the garage and she will go get him. Martha is really angry now that her fear has subsided. She tells Ron to get home immediately and that she will deal with him when he arrives at home. When Ron comes in, Martha immediately tells him that the rules in the house, which he agreed to, required him to be home at 6:00. She is quite direct and tells him, "Go to your room until dinner. After dinner we will process what went on." Ron protests, "You are unfair, I didn't do anything wrong." Martha replies, "Get to your room, you are on Shut Down until after dinner." Ron is obviously furious but complies. After a rather unpleasant dinner, Martha says she is ready to talk. Ron tells his mother that two days ago he had told her about working on the school project with Wayne until 7:00. He reminds her that she was talking on the phone and he came into the room and said excuse me and asked permission to go to Wayne's the day after tomorrow to finish a science project. He said that she nodded her approval. Martha listens and does remember the incident. She

was on the telephone talking to her sister about a relationship issue and was quite
absorbed in the conversation. She vaguely remembers Ron saying something about
a science project but she thought he said that he had to call Wayne to discuss it.
Martha now has a choice. She can stonewall her son with comments like, "See
what happens when you interrupt me when I am on the telephone" or she can
admit that she misunderstood him and ask for his suggestions on how this type of
situation can be avoided in the future.

Certainly the admission that an error was made and that she is sorry that she assumed that he had broken a rule instead of first asking for an explanation will serve several purposes. First, Martha models for her son that people make honest mistakes and when they realize it, they will take responsibility for correcting them. Second, the dialogue between Martha and Ron is now problem solving oriented, involves Ron in decision-making, and shows how feedback can be used to make improve a family practice or system. Martha's admission and willingness to communicate is a good example of putting Family Centered Parenting into practice.

What do I do if my child insists on doing his homework in front of the TV?

As indicated in the last chapter, involvement with your child's homework is one of the principles of being an engaged parent. However, involvement doesn't necessarily mean that we dictate the conditions for doing homework. Children are empowered when they can successfully find, within the agreed upon standards, their own way of accomplishing their personal responsibilities. Therefore, it is appropriate to give them enough space to either succeed or realize that what they are doing is not working and that adjustments are needed.

If your child's learning style is such that having the TV on is either non-distracting or possibly even helps him/her focus homework results will reflect this fact. Negotiate the amount of time needed to complete homework and establish standards for review prior to them starting the assignment. If they meet the standards in the specified time frame than there is no issue. If they aren't successful, then there is clear evidence that the TV approach is not effective and that they must find a different way to meet the homework standards. If the chosen behavior (TV watching) proves ineffective a new choice is evidently required. This choice flows from a natural comparison of results with goals rather than an imposition by parents. This process meets needs for both power and freedom without putting the parent in an overly authoritarian position.

Is it ever appropriate to use physical force against my child?

There are very limited times where physical force is appropriate. The price we pay for resorting to violence to control behavior is great and is discussed in detail in a previous chapter. However, when it comes down to protecting ourselves or our children from harm it might be the only alternative. For example, if a child is throwing objects at someone or hitting a parent or sibling, it is certainly reasonable and necessary to physically intervene. It is important that the intervention should be defensive in nature and be as short in duration as possible. As an illustration let us imagine that we come upon a ten-year-old punching a younger brother. If the child does not immediately respond to a verbal command to stop, wrapping our arms around the child and holding on to them until they calm down is defensive and appropriate. On the other hand if we intervene by delivering a slap in the face or a hard shove we are engaging in an offensive action which is always unacceptable.

It should be noted that after a physical interaction it is essential for the parent and child to process what happened. The child should work through the problem solving model to help him/her understand the reasons and consequence for the choices s/he made in acting violently, how to make restitution for losses caused by the behavior and to prepare a plan to meet his/her needs in a more appropriate manner.

As a child gets older, the ability to physically intervene becomes more and more problematic. In the case of a threatening or out of control teenager a verbal choice should be presented which gives the child the option of calming down or the parent calling the police for assistance. As difficult as it seems, there are times where the natural consequence for a violent outburst is the involvement of law enforcement personnel.

How can Family Centered Parenting strategies help a family that is about to move to a new community?

Regardless of their age or grade going to a new school can be frightening and stressful for children. The process of changing schools as a result of a family move is fraught with anxiety and uncertainty. How that stress is managed will often dictate the success of the experience. Therefore, parents must take concrete steps to insure that the transition is smooth, positive and framed in such a way that the children will appreciate the exciting aspects of the change.

First and foremost is to listen to the children and validate their concerns and fears. Keep in mind that for children a change in home and school is a threat to their fundamental sense of security and safety. When a child's physical environment is seriously altered his/her sense of control-power is sharply diminished. Furthermore, to the child and realistically also to the parent, there are real losses associated with a move. Leaving a home that has been structured to meet your needs coupled with the separation from friends and neighbors are legitimate loses that must be acknowledged. Effective listening provides an opportunity to for these feelings to be expressed and heard. The recognition of the feelings of loss provided by the parents helps to restore the child's diminished sense of power before inappropriate behaviors come into play. As discussed in Chapter 2 listening does not mean you have to agree that all of the feelings are appropriate, just that they are real for the child and understood. The listening phase should be followed by a discussion stressing the positive aspects of the move. Make a point to elicit all the potential benefits which might include better location, a newer school, an improved curriculum, the potential to meet new friends, especially when there has been insufficient number of peers with compatible interests, more recreational opportunities and improved family economic conditions. The positives should be presented alongside the losses so that the child learns that decision making is really a weighing of pro's and con's and not the attainment of a perfect solution. This is an important life lesson to model for children.

The next step in the process is to take an active role in planning the educational program in your child's new school. Make sure that school records from the previous school are sent in a timely fashion. Visit the school and ask to meet with and an administrator or, in the case of a high school, with the guidance counselor. Let school personnel know who you are and that you are a concerned and knowledgeable consumer of educational services. Give them placement information that is based on your unique perspective as a parent and might not be apparent in regular school records. Make suggestions about teacher or team placement that is based on your child's past experiences. Find out about deadlines and criteria for qualifying for programs such as Gifted & Talented, Honors, Advanced Placement, Basic Skills Instruction or other needs, which might include special education, speech and handicap access.

If at all possible, provide your child with actual imagery about the new school. Visit the school or at least see the school from the outside as early in the moving process as feasible. It is especially critical for younger children to have images of the new place to help them dispel fears about the unknown.

Finally, plan the farewell. The leave-taking ritual is important in helping a transition go smoothly. Discuss with your child the options for communication with the friends they are leaving behind. Use the challenge of communication as a positive experience by updating or buying a new computer to be used for email or starting a journal to memorialize the moving experience.

Moving is a challenging experience for a family. However, like many of life's challenges, with the right preparation and strategies the whole family can learn and grow from this passage.

Does Family Centered Parenting work with younger children?

The choice theory explanation of needs operates in all of us regardless of age. Young children make choices to have their needs met. In that sense, viewing young children from this perspective is helpful in guiding parental interventions. Obviously, the developmental level of the child will certainly influence the type of interventions we use. A three year old is not going to complete a plan sheet and be able to process fully the needs they were meeting by a particular behavior. However, children from about five years old and up can understand their basic needs if explained using very concrete and straightforward examples. A family meeting, based on the attention span of a child, can be undertaken with children starting at age three. Although a child this age might not fully understand aspects of the discussion, the overall experience of sitting attentively and watching parents and older siblings interact is an important model for that child's future behavior.

The other benefit of starting early is the establishment of patterns of communication and models for problem solving. Even though a three year old child might not fully understand that a particular negative behavior is need fulfilling and a choice. By the parent using the Family Centered Parenting vocabulary to explain to the child what is happening, the parent is setting the tone for the future when the child will have the cognitive ability to make sense of this approach and it will then be a lot easier to implement Family Centered Parenting.

In general, younger children—ages two to four—benefit from the following strategies:

- ✓ *Do not rely on saying no. Young children do not fully comprehend that no means stop the behavior. Instead, divert the child with an alternative activity.*

- ✓ *Do not repeat the same command over and over. Children become conditioned to ignoring the repetition and then only respond when the parent either raises their voice or intervenes in a different way.*

- ✓ *Ask a child, when they are sufficiently verbal, "What are you doing?" followed by, "Is that the way we practiced?" This pre-supposes that certain simple behavioral rules have been explained and illustrated to the child.*

How do I handle a hot topic discussion at a family meeting when the subject might not be appropriate for a younger child in the family?

There are times when the scope and details of a particular topic might not be suitable for a younger child in the family. Parents should make the decision if a topic gets too specific for a particular child. When the child's participation in the meeting is no longer appropriate the parents should excuse the child from the meeting with an explanation that what will be discussed is meant for their older sibling(s). Good practice would be to begin the discussion at a level that is appropriate for all of the children and then when the parents judge that the scope of the discussion is no longer suitable they should then excuse the child that is not of sufficient maturity to participate. For example, if the topic being discussed is sexuality and the family's value is abstinence it would be appropriate for all of the children to discuss the broader reason for abstinence. However, if the discussion then leads to helping a teenager set limits about intimacy with a boyfriend or girlfriend this might be the time to excuse the younger child(ren). It must be emphasized that there are no strict age guidelines for a parent to follow. Parents need to make a decision about exclusion based on the maturity and ability to comprehend of their own children. It is not recommended that this be done too often since excluding a child from a family meeting is contrary to the purpose of family meetings.

What adjustments do I make in parenting a teenager?

As mentioned earlier, Family Centered Parenting takes into account the changes in the dynamics of a family as the children develop. As long as individual needs are respected as they evolve, effective communication principles are followed and family meetings are held on a regular basis there is no necessity to modify Family Centered Parenting practices. However, since most parents face their greatest challenges parenting adolescents there are some ideas that should be stressed:

✓ *Effective Communication Rule #1—Seek to understand before being understood is especially critical when dealing with your teenager. Teenagers tend not to* read another person's emotional state very accurately and are prone to extreme mood swings. Before a parent offers advice or suggests solutions it is crucial to acknowledge that what your teenager is experiencing emotionally is real for them.

✓ Adolescence, by definition, is a time of testing boundaries and rules. Therefore, active negotiation about curfews, privileges and personal freedom must take place within the structure of regular family meetings and as specific issues become critical. Negotiation is not a dirty word and can lead to win-win problem solving where both parent and child's needs are met.

✓ Teenager's schedules are usually cluttered with numerous activities and demands for their time. This is particularly challenging for the adolescent since organizational skills are not fully developed at this age. Therefore, setting aside time during the family meeting to plan schedules and to adopt the use of electronic calendars to implement schedules are extremely helpful.

✓ Remind yourself that you were once a teenager and did walk in your child's shoes. Think back to the times during those years when you felt confused, vulnerable and pressured and think what was and what would have been helpful to you. Keep this in your mind when dealing with this turbulent time in your child's life.

So many parenting books suggest behavior modification, what does Family Centered Parenting have to say about behavior mod?

Essentially, the principles underlying behavior modification are in conflict with "Choice Theory," the foundation of Family Centered Parenting. Behavior modification is coercive and relies on external reinforcers rather than internal responsibility to shape a child's behavior. For families, it involves a great deal of record keeping and a constant search for the new reward that is still appealing to the child. The novelty of stickers or M&M's as rewards starts to fade rather quickly. Choice Theory and behavior mod do align when it comes to giving praise. In Chapter 2, *Effective Communication Rule #7* states that we should catch our children doing something right and offer unconditional praise verbally and non-verbally (high five, pat on the back). Although technically a behavior modification technique, praising is not inconsistent with helping a child develop and internal sense of self-worth thereby increasing their power in a positive manner.

However, there are times when a **short term** behavior modification program might be helpful to jump start a child on changing a particular behavior. An illustration might be useful.

> *At a family meeting there is a discussion about healthy eating. Becky, 12 years old, reports that she is concerned with her weight and would like to lose 10 lbs. before the summer. She asks her family for suggestions to remind her to stick to her diet plan. Her brother offers an idea. If Becky weighs herself once a week in front of the family and she loses weight, the family will allow her to pick any movie to watch that night. Becky agrees.*

In this example, Becky is being externally rewarded for a behavior change. It is a form of behavior mod. However, the process followed to create The Plan is what makes this approach acceptable. Becky brought up the issue at a family meeting and asked for help. She did not have this imposed upon her. A member of her family made a suggestion which Becky found acceptable because the reward was consistent with her need for fun and love and belonging with her family. In addition, The Plan is narrow in focus, does not require a great deal of record keeping and most importantly involves the entire family.

The conclusion is that behavior mod is a tool that under limited circumstances can have some use in bringing positive behavior change.

How do I monitor my child's use of the computer, cell phone, etc.?

It is important to remember that the fundamental principles concerning regulating behavior does not change to accommodate a particular behavior. The process is what is most important. The family meeting should be the forum for establishing rules concerning the use of technology. Utilizing effective communication principles each member of the family needs to be heard and have their input respected as the rules are negotiated and set in place. Remember, rules are easier to enforce when they reflect the values of the individual and there is a sense of ownership in the process of setting those rules. If the rule is not followed, then The Plan intervention is imposed with shutdown utilized if the child does not engage in The Plan process.

An illustration would be useful.

At a family meeting, Melissa, 14, and Kevin, 12, are again asking their parents, Stan and Ellen, for internet connection to their laptop computers. Up to now there has been one computer connected to the internet in family room and it has allowed the adults to monitor use. The children do have laptops without internet connections for doing homework and writing reports. The children raise a number of reasons for being able to be on-line. School work does require internet research and they often are doing homework at the same time. In addition, in the evenings, at times, Stan does need to go online to check late work emails further tying up the family computer. Stan and Ellen voice their concern: excessive time, access to inappropriate web sites and social network abuse, and ask Melissa and Kevin how the parental concerns can be addressed. The children are then given a week to come back with a plan at the next meeting.

The following week Melissa and Kevin present their ideas. The solution essentially relies on trusting the children to do the right thing with a few novel ideas. For example, the children offer to place their laptops outside of their bedroom doors at 10:30 each night (the time Stan and Ellen usually turn in) to insure that they are not staying up too late because of computer use. After some research, Ellen found filtering software that gives parents the ability to control and monitor a child's use of the Internet, irrespective of where the parents are, in the neighboring room, at work, or even on vacation, thus enabling parents to protect their children from the dangers of the Internet. Stan and Ellen make it clear that the parental control software is a necessary part of their plan and explain their reasons. All members agree to accept the solution and it is put in writing and signed by everyone. Stan and Ellen remind the children that there is no excuse for violating the agreement and that The Plan will be utilized if a rule is broken.

It should be noted that in this particular example Family Centered Parenting has been in place for some time and the children and parents both find the process need fulfilling. In addition, there is a trust factor involved because as we know no matter how close we inspect our children the potential for abuse exists. However, we need to come to terms with the fact that much of what are children do, especially as they become teenagers, is not subject to close inspection and we rely on the values that have been instilled through family meetings, discussion of hot topics and a strong sense of responsibility that we have helped develop.

Summary

The Family "P.E.A.C.E" tree serves as a good visual reminder of what Family Centered Parenting is all about. The acronym, PEACE, stands for *P*arent *E*mpowerment *A*nd *C*hild *E*mpowerment the foundation for a healthy, connected and joyful family life. As first mentioned in Chapter 3, the PEACE tree contains all of the elements of the Family Centered Parenting program. At the bottom of the drawing are the roots of the tree. Roots bring the essential nutrients (ingredients) to sustain the life of the tree and anchor it the environment. The three main roots of Family Centered Parenting are family values, individual needs and the principles of effective communication.

Clarifying and living a family's unique values anchors the family. A family's values are the greatest asset in maintaining stability in an environment where we are bombarded by instant media, social networks and a multitude of mixed messages to our children about right and wrong.

Understanding and expressing the individual needs of all members of a family builds the connections between family members while allowing individuals to be respected and understood—the essence of personal power. Focusing attention on what we need is the only way we can build consensus without diminishing other members of the family.

Effective communication principles are so essential to the vitality of the family that if they are ignored the PEACE tree would certainly die. Communication is not a strategy unto itself. It is the means to implement the strategies of Family Centered Parenting. If family members do not communicate effectively, it is impossible to use the tools needed to build the cohesive family unit we all strive for.

The roots meet the trunk of the tree—the family meeting. When family values are clarified and individual needs are expressed following effective communication principles then the family is ready to use the family meeting to establish and fulfill its mission and values. The mission and values are the base for the limbs of the tree to grow.

The limbs are the tools to help the family interact with the world around them. Problem solving and education are the two main limbs and provide structure for the smaller specific branches that help us deal with the day to day needs of the family.

Finally, the fruits of the tree are its leaves. When the tree is healthy, the leaves are the byproduct—Parent Empowerment And Child Empowerment—PEACE.

The P.E.A.C.E. tree can be found at
www.GrowingGreatRelationships.com

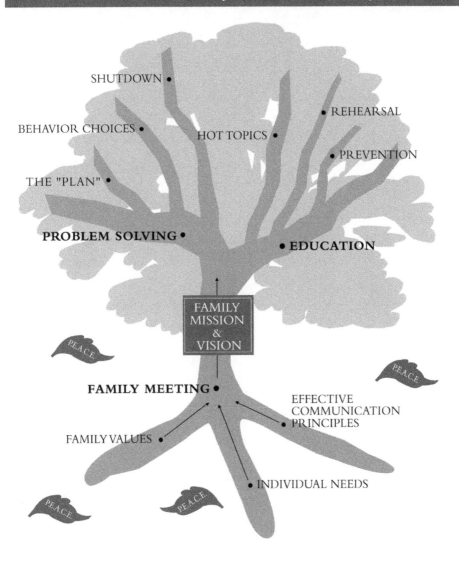

FAMILY CENTERED PARENTING®
P.E.A.C.E. Tree ➡ Parent Empowerment And Child Empowerment

About the Author

Richard C. Horowitz, Ed.D.

D r. Richard Horowitz and his wife, Jane, are partners in Growing Great Relationships, a relationship and parenting coaching practice. Having earned a Doctorate in Education from Rutgers University, for over 40 years Dr. Horowitz has taught and been in senior administration in both public and private schools, directed a non-profit serving families with children with serious behavioral health issues, has served as faculty at several universities and is group facilitator, trustee and past-president for Men Mentoring Men. He is a highly sought after speaker for local and national workshops and seminars concerning parenting, special education, fathering and family systems and is a frequent contributor to online parenting sites, radio and talk shows. He and his wife are parents of six children and two grandchildren.

Bibliography

Covey, S.R. (1989). The 7 habits of highly effective people, New York: Simon & Schuster.

Covey, S.R. (1997). The 7 habits of highly effective families, New York: Golden Books.

Glenn, H.S. & Nelsen, J. (1987). Raising children for success, California: Sunrise Press.

Glasser, W. (1965). Reality Therapy, a new approach to psychiatry, New York: Harper & Row.

Glasser, W. (1998). Choice Theory, New York: HarperCollins.

Gossen, D. C. (1993). Restitution, restructuring school discipline, North Carolina: New View Publications.

Hoy, W. K. & Miskel, C. G. (1978). Educational Administration: Theory research, and practice, New York: Random House.

Sheehy, G. (1996). New passages: Mapping your life across time, New York: Ballantine Books.

BUY A SHARE OF THE FUTURE IN YOUR COMMUNITY

These certificates make great holiday, graduation and birthday gifts that can be personalized with the recipient's name. The cost of one S.H.A.R.E. or one square foot is $54.17. The personalized certificate is suitable for framing and will state the number of shares purchased and the amount of each share, as well as the recipient's name. The home that you participate in "building" will last for many years and will continue to grow in value.

Here is a sample SHARE certificate:

THIS CERTIFIES THAT
YOUR NAME HERE
HAS INVESTED IN A HOME FOR A DESERVING FAMILY

1985-2005

TWENTY YEARS OF BUILDING FUTURES IN OUR
COMMUNITY ONE HOME AT A TIME

1200 SQUARE FOOT HOUSE @ $65,000 = $54.17 PER SQUARE FOOT
This certificate represents a tax deductible donation. It has no cash value.

YES, I WOULD LIKE TO HELP!

I support the work that Habitat for Humanity does and I want to be part of the excitement! As a donor, I will receive periodic updates on your construction activities but, more importantly, I know my gift will help a family in our community realize the dream of homeownership. **I would like to SHARE in your efforts against substandard housing in my community!** *(Please print below)*

PLEASE SEND ME _____ SHARES at $54.17 EACH = $ $_____

In Honor Of: _____

Occasion: (Circle One)   HOLIDAY   BIRTHDAY   ANNIVERSARY

    OTHER: _____

Address of Recipient: _____

Gift From: _____ *Donor Address:* _____

Donor Email: _____

I AM ENCLOSING A CHECK FOR $ $_____ PAYABLE TO HABITAT FOR HUMANITY OR PLEASE CHARGE MY VISA OR MASTERCARD *(CIRCLE ONE)*

Card Number _____ Expiration Date: _____

Name as it appears on Credit Card _____ Charge Amount $ _____

Signature _____

Billing Address _____

Telephone # Day _____ Eve _____

PLEASE NOTE: Your contribution is tax-deductible to the fullest extent allowed by law.
Habitat for Humanity • P.O. Box 1443 • Newport News, VA 23601 • 757-596-5553
www.HelpHabitatforHumanity.org